advanced |
No Crying i
by Chef Miche

MW01234463

I can't begin to imagine how many lives 'Chef Michel' has touched over his expansive and celebrated cooking career. His wit, passion, and enthusiasm for all things culinary is utterly infectious. Along with the many students that came before, and after me, I will always be 'A Shoe Maker'... the cook whose food was as tough as leather! Thank you, Michel.

—*Alister Brown*
Chef/Restaurateur , Wellington, New Zealand

Chef Michel's charming memoir of how one of France's most gifted Master Chefs was created can turn any cook with a sharp knife, a pinch of sea salt, and her grandmother's frying pan into a world class chef!

—*Ellen Michaud*
author of **A Master Class: Sensational Recipes from the Chefs of the New England Culinary Institute**

I met Chef Michel more than 25 years ago when I first visited New England Culinary Institute as a young chef seeking externs for my very first kitchen brigade. I returned last year (2008) to address a graduating class and found Michel to be the same charming, energetic, and enthusiastic ambassador for NECI and his adopted home, Vermont. I can't wait to read his memoir!

Susan Spicer
Co-Founder, Bayona Restaurant, New Orleans, Louisiana

more advance praise...

It takes a very special person to imagine how to develop a unique culinary training program, then plunge in as the jack of all trades on the first day. Michel's entertaining story highlights the many twists and turns of his childhood and his professional career that culminates with the establishment of New England Culinary Institute. It is a great read and revealing of the energy, will power and optimism that has helped Michel time and again to plunge ahead into the unknown.

Fran Voigt
Co-Founder New England Culinary Institute

This is a great story of a great man. Thousands of young chefs in the US have been trained and mentored by Chef Michel, and admire and uphold his values. Definitely a spicy read for up and coming chefs, and for anyone who has a passion for product and a commitment to quality. Perfectly seasoned from a consummate professional.

Tom Bivins
Executive Chef, New England Culinary Institute
and Class of '91

No Crying in the Kitchen
A Memoir of a Teaching Chef

Michel LeBorgne
of the New England Culinary Institute

The Public Press

Randolph Caspar

For Denise —
Keep it simple.
Taste. Season. Taste
Taste.
I hope this
will bring
fun reading
Bon Appétit!

12-18-09

Permissions Department
The Public Press
100 Gilead Brook Road
Randolph, Vermont 05060.

Library of Congress Cataloging-in-Publication Data
LeBorgne, Michel.
NO CRYING IN THE KITCHEN.
I. Title.
ISBN 978-0-9764520-7-2

cover photo: Paul O. Boisvert
editing: Stephen Morris and Michael Potts
proofreading: Denise Tenzel and Alan Berolzheimer
indexing: Rochelle Elkan
book design: Michael Potts

Contents

Dedication

Most of all, to the chefs and students who have marked my life.

To my wife, Anne-Marie, for her constant support and for putting up with my craziness.

To Fran Voigt, who hired me to open New England Culinary Institute in 1980.

To Howard Fisher, who helped me keep my sanity and provided me with constant, positive feedback.

To Kay Voorhees, who graciously accepted our plea in the very early and critical days to come back to cook breakfast and lunch. She made the mission impossible possible.

To Julie Hendrickson for her constant support, advice, criticism, and her great hospitality.

To Meg Ostrum, who took the time to read the script and connected me to the Public Press.

photo credit: Paul O. Boisvert

The Scene of a Kitchen

Paris 1954, 12:00 P.M.

– *Je commande deux steaks saignant, n'oubliez pas le cresson, j'enleve une Daube.*

– *Marcel! Ce n'est pas chaud bordel, fais attention!*

– *Oui, chef.*

– *Allez magne toi le pot qu'est ce que tu as foutu hier soir?*

– *Chaud devant.*

– *Voila, t'aurai pas pu faire bien la premiére fois?*

– *Allez, allez!*

– *J'enleve un soufflé!*

Fifty years later, New York City, 2004, 11:30 A.M.

"Ordering and pickup, one Niçoise, ordering one hanger steak, medium, sauce on the side. Ordering mixed greens with duck confit, one minestrone, one beef barley, one tuna rare, one terrine, one veggie special."

Fifty years between those kitchens, but the language is the same, intensely spoken at service time. It is a symphony of organized chaos, resulting in either a masterpiece or disaster, separated by a fine line. I have lived on *both* sides of the line for the last fifty years. And I still get an adrenaline rush from wondering where I will land this time!

La Mère et le Père:
Alexandre Le Borgne and Marguerite on their wedding day, 1937

Growing Up in Brittany During the War

I was born in Lannion on the coast of Brittany before World War II to parents who were very good cooks. I can still taste my mother's *Veal Blanquette*. The classical or traditional method is to blanch the meat by dipping it in boiling water, then let it cool. The blanching process prevents decay, especially in the absence of refrigeration. My mother, however, used a different method. Instead of blanching the meat, she lightly seared it in butter. Then she added flour, water, bouquet garni, and cooked with one onion and one carrot on very low heat, barely a simmer. This is the way I make it and the way I teach students to make it.

I usually get compliments when I make veal blanquette, but honestly I do not think I have ever reached my mother's standard. Perhaps the quality of the veal, raised without hormones, was superior back then, but my mother's remarkable dish always had the same unforgettable taste.

My father's coq au Vin was superb, and you could smell it throughout the whole house. It is also difficult to duplicate today, because everything back then was organic, from the chicken to the vegetables. Portions varied slightly each time, and you used what vegetables you had in your garden. My father made *Coq au Vin* in the classical manner. He killed the chicken, then kept the blood in a jar, adding a little vinegar to prevent coagulation. The blood is added at the end, as a thickening agent for the sauce which is almost the color of dark chocolate. I prepared it this way during my apprenticeship, but now it is illegal to use the blood.

Having good cooks as parents was a good omen. Food was central to our lives, and lunch was a ritual. My father was very strict about eating on time, and I learned early that if I did not get to the table when the noon bell rang in the church tower, I would not get lunch that day.

Marguerite in 1936

My mother's name was Marguerite, but everyone called her Margot. She was a model and a seamstress. Not only was she beautiful and impeccably dressed, but she was always smiling and you could read kindness on her face. Of course I wanted some day to marry someone like her!

To watch her do dressmaking was an amazing experience. She would take a woman's measurements, throw tissue on the table, draw the specific shape or style in a blue chalk, cut the material, then baste it (not the cooking term, but to baste is to sew loosely with wide stitches). The customer then tried on the garment, my mother adding special touches and pinning it for exact fit. Her specialty was wedding gowns. Her reputation extended even to Paris, and she was very much in demand. Occasionally, she had to travel to the city, and this did not make my father happy.

My father, Alexandre, was the town postmaster and a fearless defenseman in soccer. He loved nature and, especially, to fish. I remember Sundays walking through the woods, learning about wild mushrooms and edible herbs such as wild sorrel, or ramp, a wild leek, or *pourpier*, a kind of lettuce. I learned to recognize the good mushrooms from the deadly ones. Fall was a wonderful time for chestnuts. My mother either roasted them in the fireplace or boiled them, then served them in buttermilk. They were delicious and really filled you up.

In 1943 our family moved when I was four years old to Bourg des Comptes, a small town in Brittany on La Vilaine River. This was during the German occupation of World War II. The war was from September 1939 through June 1941, and the Germans occupied France until the Armistice was signed on May 8, 1945.

We had a garden and chickens and rabbits. In the middle of the garden my father built a bomb shelter with railroad ties. Every time we heard an air raid, signaled by a siren from the church in town, we would sprint to the shelter, sometimes twice a night. We went countless times during the war. Being a child, I thought nothing of it. It was simply what we did.

Alexandre and Marguerite during World War II, 1940

The beginning of the end for the Germans came when the English bombed and leveled their submarine base at Lorient. Even miles away, we could see the sky turn red as the town and base burned.

The Germans were led to believe that the *debarquement*, or D-Day, would take place on the flat beaches near Lorient, because it would be easier for the landing craft, and the soldiers would not have to climb the cliffs of Normandy. Instead, the Allies chose Normandy where, indeed, many died in the act of liberating France. Anyone living in a free world should visit those beaches and the cemetery of those who died on D-Day. This historic ground is now owned by the United States, but maintained by the French government.

Lorient, at the end of the Brittany peninsula, was heavily guarded by the Germans in what turned out to be a tactical error. After the landing on June 6th, some U.S. troops went directly to liberate Paris. Others went south and cut off the

Germans' line of retreat. Some surrendered; some did not; but they were trapped.

It was well known locally that my father was in the F.F.I., the Forces Francaises de l'Interieur, a civilian force more commonly known as the Resistance . Called the *Maquisards* because they hid in the *maquis*, or woods, they were feared by the Germans because they could strike anywhere and at any time. Unfortunately, there were a few German sympathizers in the village. My father was aware of this and told my mother that if she found herself in a dangerous situation, she was to bring us into the *maquis* to hide with the Resistance.

One day, perhaps ten days after D-Day, I was sitting on the doorstep with my mother and another lady, Madame Lucas, whose husband was a P.O.W. My sister, Daniele, who was five months old, was in her baby carriage. Three soldiers appeared and one of them, in perfect French, demanded that my mother tell them where my father was. These soldiers did not want to surrender to the Americans and wanted to take a hostage for bargaining. As a member of the F.F.I. my father would have been a valuable bargaining chip. The head of the trio, perhaps an officer, pulled out his Lugar, pointed it at my sister, and said, "If you do not tell me where Monsieur Alexandre is, I will kill your baby and hang you on this poplar."

I started crying and could not stop, all the while looking at my little sister. The soldier was holding his shiny Lugar with a steady hand, pointed at my sister. It did not take long for my mother to decide her course of action. She told Madame Lucas to take care of my sister and me, that she would be back soon. My mother got into a car and guided the soldiers into the woods.

I knew where the Resistance headquarters was in the *maquis* because I had delivered food there. I was small and knew only about food and hungry men. The area had a dirt road on the left of a hill, and on the right were the woods filled mostly with chestnut and oak trees. I can remember the dappled light filtering through the tree leaves onto the forest floor.

My mother led the Germans to the entrance of the *maquis*,

but she also led them into an ambush, and they were killed by Resistance snipers. My mother ran back home, wrapped a few clothes in a towel, picked up my sister, and told me to follow her. She said we were going to visit some friends. I thought it strange to walk so fast through the fields when we could have taken the road, a faster, more direct route.

Forty-five minutes later we arrived at the farm of a man who played soccer with my father. His name was Jules Gicquel. It was a big farm with a stone house that had small windows, making it very dark inside. At the end of the common room was a fireplace with several cats warming themselves. The other buildings on the farm were also made of stone. There was a huge stack of cow manure mixed with hay. There were no tractors, just a small plow and the necessary implements for harvesting, and all of them horse-drawn. There was also a threshing machine, and a sickle used to collect hay into bundles, that would then be tied standing up in bunches of five or six, just like in Monet's haystack paintings.

I did not know what we were doing there, and I was tired from our long, fast walk. After dinner my mother put my sister and me in a large bed, and she laid down, holding us. When I woke up, she was gone. Madame Gicquel told me that my mother would be gone for a couple of weeks, but that I must never tell anyone that she was gone. Instead I was to say that we were on vacation from Paris and that my last name was LeMiro. *Le Miro* means you are *cock-eyed*, and my real name, *LeBorgne*, means *one-eyed*. To this day, I think this was pretty clever.

For a couple of weeks I was always asking them where my parents were, and I went to bed crying every night. During the days I played with the son of Monsieur Gicquel and the other farm kids. We had fun. Although I missed my mother terribly, playing with the boys during the day helped me forget my pain. My other vivid memory of this time is of smelling like cow manure!

The war to liberate France was raging, and my mother had joined the Maquisards. American GIs were working with the Maquisards to take advantage of their knowledge of the local

15

landscape. As postmaster my father could sneak into the post office, which also had the switchboards for all the telephones in town, and communicate with other Maquisards by phone. They did not need to worry about telephone surveillance in those days. The Resistance fighters were also in touch with de Gaulle by Morse code. Every night de Gaulle would leave coded messages on BBC radio for the Resistance fighters.

Then, one day, my mother reappeared on the farm. I can still see her as she came into sight. She was suntanned and wore a white blouse, a flowered skirt, and a pair of sandals. She was so beautiful, perhaps even more beautiful because I had missed her so much! She took us back home. Our part of France had been liberated, and the war was over! Or so we thought.

My father had put American, English, Canadian and French flags in our windows, but then one night he heard German tanks coming our way, so he took all the flags and hid them in the septic. The tanks were the last ones coming back from the Lorient front after the battles of the region were over and were trying to rejoin the German Army. I can imagine what went through my father's and mother's heads, a mixture of *Finally the war is over* and *Here we go again*. Fortunately, the Germans did not stop at our house. When they did stop at other places along the way, it was just for food, although many foot soldiers, weary from walking, stole bicycles.

When we were finally liberated officially, I remember euphoric people dancing on the street, kissing each other, changing partners, and singing… jubilation that continued non-stop for twenty-four hours. I will never forget the exhilaration and joy of our townspeople.

When you are a child, what is simply is. I did not suffer much from World War II. I remember waiting in line with my family for stamps to get a quart of milk. I remember on D-Day a gentleman we called Count Robineau rode into our backyard, jumped over the fence, and yelled to my mother, "The Americans have landed!" Then he bucked his horse and vanished, a French Paul Revere. I can see his bay horse and his leather boots. I can smell my first orange, given to me by a GI. I kept it under my pillow until it was rotten. I can see the sumptuous platters – not plates, *platters* – of sliced tomatoes, onions, buckwheat crepes, and eggs that my mother served to four handsome American GIs who came to our house in a jeep every Thursday after the Liberation.

What is simply is and what remains, remains forever.

Michel in Bourg des Comptes, 1944

Pistou

Serves 4

Prep time: 30 minutes

Cooking time: 30 minutes

The Story

Pistou is to France what Minestrone is to Italy. Often people use this soup as a base and put their final touch by adding rappini, seafood, or sausage, but don't use this to clean your leftovers from the refrigerator.

The Recipe

2 15 ounce cans cannellini beans

¼ C olive oil

2 carrots, peeled, diced ¼ "

1 purple top turnips, peeled and diced to ¼"

2 celery stalks, peeled and diced to ¼"

12 green beans, washed and cut to ½"

1 leek, white only, sliced thin

1 medium Spanish onion, slice to ¼"

1 Tbsp salt

1 ½ qt cold water

1 chef potato, peeled and diced to ¼"

2 tomatoes or ½ of 16-ounce can peeled and diced

6 garlic cloves, peeled and crushed

½ bunch basil

¼ C olive oil

In a large pot pour olive oil then add carrots, turnips, celery, green beans, leeks, onions, and salt. Cook slowly until the vegetables are tender. Add water, potato and one can of beans. Simmer until the potatoes are cooked. In a food processor, place the garlic, tomatoes and the 2nd can of beans, drained. Turn on, slowly adding olive oil, then finish with basil. Add to the soup and reheat if necessary. Serve with toasted sourdough bread.

Summers with My Grandparents

When I was seven years old and the war was over, I began spending summers with my paternal grandparents in La Prenessaye, near Loudeac in central Brittany in a small village called Le Bas des Landes, literally, *the bottom of Landes*. Only three families lived there. Many French children spent time with relatives in the country in the summer, but unlike me, most of the children who went to the country were from Paris.

I took the train from Bourg des Comptes to Rennes, where I changed trains to take the local train to La Prenessaye where my grandfather would pick me up. People in the village were impressed because I was not afraid to take the train and travel alone and would say, "Look at him! He's not afraid of anything!"

It was my job to take care of four cows and several sheep. Not knowing about cowboys then, I felt important to be corralling and taking care of animals on the ranch. The land was very poor, so my grandmother had difficulty growing vegetables. Once a week she would make a pot au feu, with all kinds of vegetables and a piece of salted pork. We would eat this two to three days in a row, until none was left. We drank hard cider with our *pot au feu*.

Twice a week the grocery truck, which was also the baker's truck, would stop, and my grandmother would buy the basic necessities, paid for with eggs, butter, and some money. She never bought coffee. I certainly wish she had, because instead of coffee we had chicory and roasted oats. It was my job to roast the oats. How I hated spending my afternoons turning the oat roaster over a wood fire! One time I got the bright idea to burn the oats, but then I realized if I burnt them, I would still have to drink the awful stuff. I loved my grandparents so much that I eventually won my mental battle and accepted the chore of roasting the oats.

My grandmother, whose name was Louise but whom I

called Mémère, was very well-read, and she insisted that I write to my parents once a week. Here is a letter I wrote when I was six or seven years old.

Le Prenessaye le 8

Dear Parents,

I am writing to you today while I am waiting to eat. I just brought back the cows. I was in "Le Petit Pre" (small field). I was with Claude my friend, who tied a stick at the tail of his dog, and when the dog ran, he was scared. I love to be with Grandma. Maman, it is cold today, can you send me another pair of pants. Last Friday I lost Pompom, my dog. I found him and gave him my sandwich. Please say hello to the Le Petit Parc and the Grand Parc. Sunday, I ate over at my godmother's and in the afternoon over at Aunt Marie's.

Big Kisses,

Michel.

Mémère et Pépère:
Pierre Le Borgne, Michel's grandfather, and his wife Marie Louise,
La Prenessaye, circa 1930

Michel's grandparents' house at Le Bas des Landes,
where he spent summers 1948-1950

My grandparents were very good to me and very loving. My grandfather, Pierre Le Borgne, was a roofer. He was only about 5'5" tall, but strong as an ox. He had an excellent reputation, spread by word of mouth, for his painstaking work. He traveled to his jobs by bicycle with his ladder strapped on. Because he did slate roofs which require exactitude, skill, and patience, he was regarded as an artisan. While he worked my grandmother tried to run the farm which was a marginal operation. I do not remember my grandparents ever taking a day off.

In the summer, my grandfather (whom we called *Pépère*) always wore a white tank top shirt and corduroy pants with suspenders. He would shave by the well, looking into a mirror nailed to a tree. When he was finished, he always asked me to kiss him to see if he had shaved closely enough. Pépère also was a smoker, as was my father who smoked two packs of Gitane, an unfiltered French cigarette, a day. Somehow, I got the idea in my head that only people who smoked had to shave!

My grandfather was one of sixteen children, but the only surviving boy. The Le Borgne line was getting smaller and smaller. He did not work on roofs on Sunday, but instead he would either cut wood for the fireplace or cut hay. One day he showed me how to set up a noose, or what is called a *collet*, to catch jack rabbits. First you bury a stick in the ground and then secure it to the noose. The trick is to put the noose at the right height. For a jack rabbit you measure by setting up one hand with the thumb up. This almost always succeeded. I caught six or seven jack rabbits during the summer, but unfortunately my dear grandmother was not a very good cook, so I have no memory of enjoying eating them. My grandfather would make wonderful slippers with the rabbit skins, and he also made a handbag for Mémère.

Every year my grandmother made some kind of moonshine by soaking currants in applejack. It must not have been very good, because one day she threw all of it in the courtyard. The chickens rushed to eat the currants. Five minutes later they were lying on their sides and we thought she had killed them, but they were just drunk. At ten years old, I thought this was pretty funny. (I still do today.)

Every morning I got up at 6:00 and washed my face in a bucket outside, next to the well. Sometimes I washed with soap, but sometimes without. Mémère made the soap by melting beef fat and *soude caustic*. I knew the name, but don't ask me what it was! She brought both ingredients to boil in a huge cast iron pot, then ladled the mixture into a rectangular mold that my grandfather had made. When it cooled, it was removed, then cut into cubes. No flower scent was added. My grandparents knew how to make use of everything!

When Mémère was too busy to make soap I just washed with cold water, followed by breakfast. My grandmother filled a large bowl – about two quarts or the size of a salad bowl – with thinly sliced stale bread, then covered this with a chicory-oats mixture, her version of *Breakfast of the Champions!*

I took my cows and my sheep two miles away from home, always accompanied by my loyal dog, Pompom, a black mutt who was very friendly and – best of all – watched cows for me. This allowed me to play with the other kids. To reward Pompom, I gave him my sandwich. Fair is fair!

The other kids, like me, were spending their summers with grandparents or other relatives. Some came from as far away as Paris. It was traditional for children from the city to spend the summer with relatives in the country, much more unusual for a boy from Brittany. My younger brother and sister never spent summers at my grandparents's home, and I have never known why. Perhaps I had too much energy and independence, but I am profoundly grateful for those summers with grandparents who were so hard-working and loving. I learned to respect work, without expecting a lot in return, from people who seemed content with their lives. Surely, there are such people today, but it is not the norm.

I summered there from the ages of eight to twelve. While my dog watched the cows, we kids played in the river and went fishing. This was also where we bathed. *Mon Dieu*, it was cold, but like so many things in life, you get used to it. No one had a watch, so we built a solar watch, with the mud and sticks. It was surprisingly effective.

Keeping track of time was important, because we needed to be home every day at noon. After a quick lunch, frequently *Paté Rillette* (a delicious paté about 95% of pork fat), tomato salad, and bread, I took a nap in the haystack with Pompom, my dog. I had to be ready at 4:00 in the afternoon to take the herd to pasture until 8:00. This was the routine seven days a week. Then afterwards, before supper, I helped my grandfather cut a big wheelbarrow of tall grass and clover for the cows. It was very heavy and we had to move it uphill, so I had to help by pulling on a rope, because it was heavy. Believe me, I did not need anything to help me sleep!

Some days, during the afternoon, I would hang around with a local character, M. Grandjien, a little bald man who was the local charcutier. A charcutier makes sausage, pate and terrine, ham, bacon, cured meat, as well as all the trimmings for the *charcroute*, sauerkraut. Mme. Grandjien was twice his size, and both of them wore big white aprons. Chatting all the time, she welcomed the customers, sold items and ran the register.

Once a week M. Grandjien killed a pig, and I helped him cut the meat. The only parts of the pig that could not be turned into food were the pigs' teeth and eyeballs. At an early age I was learning how to utilize everything in cooking.

I spent my summers in shorts and barefoot. I did not want to wear the wooden shoes made locally. With the wooden shoes I was always kicking myself in the ankle. Ouch! I was in constant discomfort, plus I did not have socks, so I had to use hay to make a very scratchy version of socks. Still, I have great memories of those summers. I even became a better reader thanks to my grandmother. I read to please her.

At summer's end my grandparents rewarded me with a piece of salt pork and a live chicken to take on the train ride home.

Ploubalay

In 1948 my father got a promotion in the postal service requiring our family to move to Ploubalay, a little town close to the English Channel which had been burned down by the Germans in 1944. It is on the coast, near St. Malo.

The post office where my father worked and our family lived was just a cold and dark house, with no running water. The only heat came from the stove and the fireplaces in the kitchen. There was an outhouse. We had a root cellar, a huge garden, chickens, and rabbits. One of my chores was killing a chicken or a rabbit every Thursday. I also had to weed the garden, which I hated. To this day, I love fresh vegetables, but I *hate* gardening.

Weeding was tedious, monotonous, and took time away from playing with my friends, whom I could hear over the wall, having a good time. There is no way anyone, even today, can talk me into gardening, because more than selecting your seeds and enjoying the harvest, gardening means *weeding*.

Every Thursday was a feast for the family. My mother would cook a whole calf's head with root vegetables, and she made a *sauce gribiche*, which is homemade mayonnaise garnished with gherkins, capers, chervil, tarragon, and chopped hard-boiled eggs.

Much later, when I was fourteen, we had a strawberry patch, and on the other side of the wall was Madame Lougen's strawberry patch. I don't know why, but her strawberries were bigger and sweeter than my father's, so once in a while I climbed over the wall which was about ten feet tall, using a ladder, and ate some strawberries. One day she saw me and told my father I was stealing her strawberries. If only she had told him I was comparing her strawberries to ours. If only someone had let me explain that I was testing the sweetness of the strawberries!

Despite the *if onlys*, my father, who was a good friend of the local gendarme, arranged to have me spend the night in the jail. Spending a night in jail at fourteen years old for stealing strawberries was harsh. In my mind this made me a jailbird. My father gave me half a loaf of bread and some water, so that I would not be able to tell any of my friends that I had been starved. It was cold, and I cried all night, looking out the small window of the cell holding the bars in the window. At seven o'clock the next morning my father came and picked me up as if nothing had happened.

But this did not stop me from playing pranks, my revenge against society. I often carried them out with my best friend, Claude LeFort, but sometimes on my own. I was the schemer, the one with the great ideas, and Claude was the executer of the prank. He was agile as a cat and could open any door, but we had our bandit ethics and never stole or broke anything. I used to be able to swallow a small frog, drink a quart of water and then spit it out, twisting my ear to add a little drama. I usually did that in front of the girls just to scare them and to get their attention! Yes, I was a show off. I stopped doing this once I realized that this stunt did not make the girls want to kiss me.

One dark night I was on my way home when I passed the church. I stopped and dropped three or four frogs in the holy water. I could just picture people going to church the following day and putting their hands in the holy water, before doing the sign of the cross! The next morning the news of the holy water spread quickly. Some people did not think it was funny and started pointing fingers. That little village was never the same.

One night, around 2 A.M., I was

Michel at 10 years old

awakened by little stones thrown at my window. It was Claude. I dressed quickly and tip-toed outside. We went to the church and poured ink in the holy water . Then we switched around the flower pots people had at their windows.

The following morning, as I walked to school, I knew we had really disturbed the village. The gendarmes were talking to the people who had been to church and to the others who could not find their flower pots. This was serious vandalism for such a small town. Some even accused the Communists of being the perpetrators of the flower pot crime!

Claude and I were always polite with everyone, especially the elderly women who were the first ones to start rumors. We would run their errands to the grocery store. To our glee, no one ever suspected us, mischievous boys that we were. If my father ever found out about it, I would have been in for a serious thrashing. Thankfully, he never did.

Our town was on the English Channel. The beaches were mined from 1939 to 1944, because the Germans did not know where or when D-Day would take place. We called the English Channel *La Manche*, and no fishing boats were allowed during the war because any outgoing boats could be headed for England. On the positive side, this five-year gap in fishing led to an abundance of seafood after the war. My father or mother would say "Michel, go get lunch (or dinner)." A half an hour later, I had abalone, shrimp, cockles, conger eel and sometimes lobster. Where there is conger eel, there is lobster, because the eels feed on the lobsters when their shells turn soft.

There was also crab, octopus, and squid. From the rocks I picked periwinkle, a small black snail. In France, snails were – and are – served in a bar with a cork filled with pins. You use the pins to pick out the snails. They are delicious! At high tide I sat at the end of the pier with my bucket and fishing pole. It seemed every time I cast, I would catch a fish – mackerel, whiting, bass, many more. Twenty minutes later the fish was in the frying pan, or poached, or turned into a *cotriade*, which is a poor man's fish soup.

This is when I acquired my great love of fresh fish. This is not what we call "fresh" today. The trawler might have just docked in Boston but has been at sea for two weeks. Interestingly, fresh fish does not smell fishy. Fresh fish smells like cucumber.

High School in Plancoet

From ages twelve to fifteen I went to *Cours Complementaire de Plancoet*, a central high school. There were no buses, and Plancoet was twelve kilometers away from home, so we all bicycled from our different villages. My friends, Claude Le-Fort and Bernard Merdrignac, bicycled from Ploubalay; Louis Georgennet from Tregon; Joel Pillard from St. Jacut; and the le Lievre brothers from Notre Dame du Guildo. We rode together in small packs, rain or shine. I do not remember much snow, but it could be windy – very windy – and cold. Despite the intense exposure and a winter wind that could cut right through you, I do not recall ever being sick or missing a day of school.

Two or three nights a week we raced bicycles, village to village. I won almost every night. Claude and Bernard would lead the pack on the flats, and then I pedaled quickly in the uphill of Crehen. Some of the boys were able to follow, some not, but it was on the last sprint where I would win. If you follow the Tour de France, it is similar because the last leg of the race is all uphill. All my friends were telling me to join a local cycling club, but my father was absolutely opposed to my racing. It was not that I was thinking about becoming a professional at fifteen, I just wanted to race – against anyone! I had a burning desire to compete, win or lose. During the spring we organized races up to sixty kilometers (about forty miles). There were about twenty-five competitors, and we raced for the sake of racing. No prizes, no trophies, just the challenge and reward of seeing how far you can push yourself. It probably didn't hurt that my father was so strongly against it!

While I was a fierce bicycle racer, I was only an average student. Perhaps the reason my father discouraged me from racing was because, at that time, only "bums" were racing. This was not considered a real sport, and those who pursued it were non-conformists, outside the mainstream. To not be able to compete was one of the biggest disappointments in my life. Who knew? One of the guys I used to beat was Desire LeTort, who became France's champion and who raced the Tour de France several times! I will never know what would have happened if my career had been in bicycling instead of cooking.

Thursday, a day off from school in Ploubalay, was a special day for generations of kids from the private Catholic school who wanted to fight the kids from the public school. Don't ask me why, it was just a stupid tradition, perhaps akin to a rivalry here between prep school kids and townies. We made our swords out of wood, bows and arrows, but our ultimate weapons were the sling shots we made with rubber bands from tire tubes. My friend Claude was very good with his sling shot and could kill blackbirds with it. The fights were violent, but not lethal. The following day you could feel your bruises.

On Thursday, if I was not fighting the Catholic kids – we called them *les chouans* – I was delivering bread with Victor Hervy. Victor was in his mid-thirties and was the local *boulanger*, along with his father, also Victor, but in his early sixties. Their bread was the best country bread I have ever eaten. Baking was a labor of love for the Hervys. Victor – *père* and *fils* – did not have a fancy retail shop. Why bother? Most of the bread was sold before it came out of the oven.

The boulangerie had a low ceiling, probably made this way for a better, more natural, proofing of the bread. Proofing is when the dough "rests" before going in the oven. At the end of the boulangerie was the wood fired oven, and to the right of the oven was a big table with two benches. The table was covered by newspapers and magazines with a bottle of hard cider and country paté with a knife stabbed into it, and, of course, a loaf of delicious, crusty bread. The other end of the room was stacked with bags of flour, with several napping cats in case of a wandering mouse. No need for fancy mousetraps.

Victor and Victor were unusual for the fact that they slept until 7 A.M., like most people, but not most bakers. They did not believe in getting up at midnight to have the bread ready first thing in the morning. Nor did they make croissants and baguettes for the breakfast crowd. They made only large, round, six- to eight-pound *miche*, a bread that needs at least two days to age before it can be sliced. Unlike other bread, it keeps for seven to ten days before becoming stale. This bread had no additives, only flour, sea salt, spring water, and the starter. (The starter is bread dough set aside to rise between six to eight hours at room temperature.)

Their bread was ready by two o'clock in the afternoon. Victor Junior would nap while his father stacked the bread in the carriage and prepared the horse. By four o'clock Victor, the son, had eaten his lunch and was ready to deliver bread (after putting a bottle of hard cider in the carriage. No Evian!) As five o'clock rang from the church tower, the horse slowly started walking.

I always asked Victor if he needed company. He did not need help, but he wanted someone to listen to his stories. He delivered bread five days a week with five different routes. The deliveries took four to five hours. I do not know if it was profitable to deliver, but it was a good gesture. Victor also delivered packages at no charge and transferred messages from one farmer to another. On Sundays there was no delivery as farmers came to the boulangerie to pick up their bread after Mass. The Victors did not make bread on Monday.

The horse did not need any guidance – he knew all the routes and the stops. Victor knew exactly how much bread each farm needed. If no one was home, often the case especially in the summer, the bread was left behind the shutters and the money collected from the flower pot. The bread customers always left the exact change.

Victor's stories were about traditions in Brittany, World War II, and the village. There were some funny ones, but some I did not understand. Still I laughed loudly. I did not want to be a boring rider.

In summer those Thursday deliveries went fast. In winter Victor would look for me. I knew it could be a long, lonely, cold day so I went with him whenever possible. Victor always had hot cider and a sheepskin blanket. When the deliveries were over, I helped Victor brush and feed the horse, then went home and directly to bed. I was not hungry, having eaten bread all afternoon, not to mention drinking cider. No sleeping pills were needed.

I started work very early in my life. Ar twelve or thirteen

years old I was picking green beans in the summertime for some of the farmers nearby. I also was a golf caddy, even though I never played golf. I was not the kind of kid to read books at the beach and work on a suntan. I had to do something physical and challenging, to make use of my energy. I had more than I knew what to do with.

My Entrance into the Food Industry

I started in the food industry as a bartender's helper at age fourteen in the summer of 1953. I biked to Dinard, nine kilometers from home, to find a job. Anything would do. First, I tried at Le Pengouin, an extremely busy brasserie, but the owner, Fernand, thought that I was too young, and that it would be too difficult for me too keep up with washing all the dishes. Then I went to Hotel Roche Corneil, because I had been told they were looking for a bell boy. Unfortunately, by the time I arrived, they had just filled the position, but they told me that the Hotel des Dunes, just across the street, was looking for a bell boy. I ran there and met the owner, Monsieur Combs, a well-dressed gentleman, who told me that he had just filled their bell boy position.

I was determined and would not take no for an answer. I was not going home before I could secure a job for the summer. I asked Monsieur Combs if he might have a position in the kitchen washing pots or doing prep work. "I will do anything," I said to him, then thought, "Oh my God, I hope he does not say gardening!" He looked me over closely, from head to toe. I had made it a point to be impeccably clean.

"Do you speak English?"

"No, sir," I answered, but continued looking at him straight in the eyes, hoping he could see how determined I was.

"Well, you are a little young, but would you like to work as a helper in the bar and help the sommelier bring the wine from the cellar?" Then he added, "You know it is long hours."

"Yes, sir! School ends June 15, and I can be here June 16."

He brought me into his office and told me more about my job responsibilities. I would have room and board. I forget the salary, but the job was for two and a half months with no days off. That's how it was in 1953.

I returned home triumphant, telling my parents I had found a job for the summer at the four-star hotel that had once been a palace in Dinard. I needed two pairs of black pants, four white shirts, two pairs of comfortable, well-designed black shoes, and a black bow tie. They provided the white coat. It was close to Easter, which gave my mother ample time to make my pants and shirts.

The last day of school I packed my little suitcase and strapped it to my bike. The next day I got up early and biked to Dinard. As I rode, I worried where I could store my prized bike at the hotel. When I arrived, a bell boy, Gigi (short for Gilles), showed me my room, or I should say "our" room, because we were to be roommates for the summer. The room was dark with basic necessities – one hand sink and two closets. I was still nervous about where to park my bike, but Gigi saved the day. He showed me the storage room, where they stored china, glasses and silver. It was cleaner than our room and certainly had more light. This room was secure as a safe in a bank, because Gigi was the only employee with a key! This was a huge relief.

Gigi was eighteen, and it was his third year working at the hotel. His job was similar to that of a concierge. He was a very funny guy who could imitate anyone, and knew how to talk to the ladies. He also made unbelievable tips.

Next, I met Marie-Thé, the woman in charge of the bar. I was only fourteen, but I knew when I was facing a beautiful woman. She was twenty-five years old, tall, blonde, blue eyed and had a beautiful smile. She was a natural beauty who never wore make-up, except lipstick, and always wore high heels while working. She was a graduate of L'Ecole Hotelière de Grenoble, a culinary school where you elect your major in the third year. She had picked Front of the House, Maître d'Hôtel, Bartender, Sommelier and Table Service.

She gave me a blue apron and showed me my duties, using a checklist. This was not a bar where people hung around and watched TV. It was two cozy, well-decorated rooms. I was to cover the one with the piano and a big window overlooking the terrace, my own territory. The customers at the hotel were mostly English aristocrats.

31

To my great surprise, M. and Mme. Combs had me sit at lunch with them, their daughter Jacqueline, and M. Louis, the maître d'hôtel. We were served by the wait staff. The lunch lasted forty-five long minutes, and I was on edge, because I'm sure they were examining my table manners.

After lunch, I went to my room to dress up, clean and comb my hair. I entered the bar and Marie-Thé told me to go back to the hallway where she inspected me from shoes to shirt to fingernails. I passed the inspection, and told myself "Michel, don't mess with this woman ... she is serious."

Gigi gave me the inside scoop on everything. He explained that the reason I had eaten with the boss and not with the employees was to protect my virgin ears from their swearing and off-color stories. If only they had known, I had heard plenty of both on the street.

Marie-Thé was the top barmaid in town. Her name was a shortened version of Marie-Thérèse. All the hotels wanted to hire her because she knew her drinks, but also because she brought in the right crowd. She wore a serious expression, as a way of protecting herself, because all the guys in town had fantasies of being the lucky one to take her home.

The first day was spent observing what went on in the bar. The second day Marie-Thé showed me more than I could remember – how to make espresso and tea with tea leaves, how to present myself, how to take an order, how to carry a tray, walk like a ballet dancer, not as if I were pushing a plow! After lunch we sat down, and she told me the tricks of the trade, such as asking to refill the glass before it was empty and then charging for a full glass.

First, she told me, I must find out which people were staying in the hotel. She received a list from Gigi with comments about the return customers – who was friends with whom, their favorite drinks, the good tippers, and the bad ones. This was an essential list.

Gigi was *la boîte à lettres,* which literally means the mailbox. People gave him secret notes to be discretely delivered, so Gigi had the book on everyone. This was why he made so much in tips!

Shortly after I arrived, I confessed to Gigi that I did not think I was doing a good job. "Listen," he told me, "you are here for two days, and you want to know everything. Marie-Thé is going to drive you crazy for one week just to find out what you are made of." Gigi was right. I began to feel more confident waiting on tables, and never had to be reminded to pick up the complimentary hors d'oeuvres and chips from the kitchen.

I was drawn to the kitchen, its ambience, the camaraderie, the energy, the smell of the food, plus Chef Pierrot gave me new food to try. After two weeks Marie-Thé sat me down and gave me a review, touching on my good points and areas where I needed to improve, like my English. She gave me more responsibility and also changed my schedule. I would now do the opening – cleaning the bar, stocking the liquor, wine, and beer, ice, coffee, tea – and she would do the closing. We would alternate a three-hour break in the afternoon, because we were not both needed all day. At break I sometimes went to the beach, other times biking home via the scenic route on the coast. During the Tour de France I mimicked a reporter's commentary as if I were riding in the Tour. "Here is Le Borgne, the yellow jersey, leading the chase ..."

Another reason I went home was to show my father how much money I was earning. I needed to prove my success to him. At the hotel I had become familiar with many customers, so that I knew their preferences, such as their favorite seats. I would put a reserved sign on the table for those customers. Under the guidance of Gigi and Marie-Thé, I learned the dos and don'ts of the trade. The summer was going by fast. What little spare time I had, perhaps two or three times a week, was spent on rigorous bike rides, pushing myself up steep hills because I wanted to be in top shape when school resumed.

When that time came, it was like saying goodbye to family. Monsieur Combs asked me if I would like to come back the next year.

"Yes sir, I would love to." I also asked him to keep me in mind for a kitchen position. He reached into his pocket and gave me a roll of money. It was the first time someone had acknowledged my hard work, and it made me feel great.

When I said goodbye to Marie-Thé, she gave me a big hug and kiss on the cheek. I felt very much the little brother. She had taught me so many nuances of the hospitality business – how not to cut in on a conversation, how to be polite, how to be visible without being seen. Her perfume had a very sensual scent. To this day, I could detect that perfume in a ballroom full of people. We promised to stay in touch. She told me that she was heading to Chamonix in the Alps for the winter season.

I returned home on my bike with my dirty laundry, and my head in the clouds.

About a month after I arrived home I told my father I wanted to go to a cooking school. "So, no more biking for you?" he said.

"I already won the Tour de France. I want to retire on top."

He did not appreciate my humor.

The week before Easter, Marie-Thé called me. She had returned from Chamonix and was calling to find out if I could help during the Easter weekend. No problem! At the end of the weekend, however, she told me that she was not returning for the summer. She did not go into details, but I think she left to make more money elsewhere.

I was devastated, not only because Marie-Thé was not returning, but also because I was sure they would ask me to run the bar until they found her replacement. I wanted to work in the kitchen.

I guessed right about running the bar, but c'est la vie. Monsieur Combs gave me a raise, but my heart was in the kitchen with Chef Pierrot, even though we had yet to work together. An older gentleman replaced Marie-Thé in the bar. He was good, but he couldn't shine her shoes. I tried to make the best of it because by now I had my own clientele of hotel guests and was making a good living. Also, I now ate with all the employees, which was much more fun!

At the end of the season, several of us got together at Le Pengouin to celebrate with French fries and drinks – Orangina for me. Around midnight Marie-Thé showed up, a surprise for all of us. I was as excited as a little kid in front of the Christmas tree. She asked about my summer, and I told her that soon I was going to a cooking school in Tours. She told me if I ever needed anything, even money, to get in touch with her. I believe she was sincere, but that was the last time I saw Marie-Thé. Many times I have thought about her, what she taught me, how she brought me along, her interest in my life and dreams. Nothing else in the world meant more to me.

Grilled Duck Breast Jean Louis

Serves 4

Prep time: 20 minutes

Cooking time: 30 minutes

The Story

I learned a lot while working at "Saigon" in Aix en Provence under the supervision of Jean Louis Amiand. Most of my light dishes come from my stay at "Saigon". I also learned how to grill duck breast a different way.

The Recipe

4 Duck breasts, boneless
1 C granulated sugar
1½ C water
½ C Nuoc nam (fish sauce)
1 Tbsp Garlic, chopped
2 Tsp coarse black pepper
4 oranges for juice or ¾ cup
Fresh mint for garnish
1 cucumber, peeled, seeded, sliced

Place sugar and ½ C of water in sauce pot. Cook until it reaches a caramel color, remove from the fire and add 1 C of water. Be careful not to burn yourself. Let cool and add the remaining ingredients except the mint and cucumber. Pour over the duck breasts to marinate for a minimum of three hours. Dry the duck breasts and tie two breasts together, skin side out. Place on broiler on medium and cook the breasts slowly. The fat should be crispy and medium rare is recommended. Let the meat rest. Reduce the marinade; adjust the taste by adding a little balsamic vinegar. Untie the duck breasts, slice on the bias. Attractively place the meat on the plate with basmati rice. Ladle with sauce. Garnish with mint and cucumber slices.

My Apprenticeship Begins

In September of 1954, at the age of fifteen, just three days after returning from my summer job at the Hotel des Dunes, I entered the Centre d'Apprentissage de Tours, one of the best cooking schools in France. Tours is a city in the Loire Valley. The reason that my father chose that school was it was a boarding school with a reputation as being strict. My father thought I was too headstrong and needed to be "broken in."

There were few cooking schools in France then. Others were in Strasbourg, Grenoble, and Nice. Tours was the closest to Brittany. Had I not been accepted there, my father would have arranged to have me fishing for cod in Newfoundland. Two to three months at a time in the cold, gray North Atlantic? No bicycle, no girls, no friends? Day after day of flopping codfish? *No, thanks*, I thought, *if it comes to that, I will run away.* My father and I had vastly different views of what I should do with my life. I had enough experience with my summer jobs to reach the conclusion that my future was in the kitchen.

Before I left, I said goodbye to my bike, after polishing it to a nice shine. It was a Petit Breton brand and a wonderful dark green. My bike was my best friend and my companion. We had so much fun together. Bicycling had carried me through many hard times and opened the door for new experiences, not to mention taking me to new places.

My father drove me to the train at Plancoet, the town of my school and many bike races. I waved goodbye from inside the train. He waved back from the platform. It took place in slow motion, because it was a goodbye to the world of my father and his rules, and the beginning of a long, hard climb up the ladder of the culinary world. This would be my world, and I felt both scared and excited.

At the school we slept forty in a dormitory, just like the movie, *Les Choiristes*, and had no hot water to wash our faces. We

Michel and his sister, Daniele, in Lamballe, 1954

showered on Thursdays, with someone timing us to be out of the shower in two or three minutes. The school ran from Monday to Friday, plus half a day on Saturday. We alternated between general education and cooking and pastry classes.

There were seventeen in my particular class. Several are now in North America including Jean-Charles Berruet, who owns The Chanticleer in Nantucket; Marcel Keraval, who owns Café de France in St. Louis; my best friend, Claude Coeuret, who now has a catering business in Québec City; and Denis Floch, who owns My Bretagne in Florida.

Despite its reputation for tight discipline, school was not too bad, although I chafed for more freedom. I figured out that if you were a good rugby player you could have some extra privileges, such as a shower after practice! And if you were good enough, you could play in the town on the weekend, where you could stay overnight.

I had never played rugby. In Brittany you either bicycled or played soccer. Even though I was fast, I was not a good soccer player, because I did not have good ball control skills. Despite my lack of experience, I joined the school rugby team with the great desire to learn the sport, but an even greater desire to escape the dorm on weekends. #10 was my number and fly half my position. I was fifteen years old, 5'6" tall, 155 pounds, with a reputation as a lean, mean, fast machine.

Rugby is a brutal sport, played by gentlemen. It came easily to me, just like cooking, because I had both vision and passion. The first year I was voted not the best, but the most improved player. I caught the attention of the school superintendent, who was the president of U.S. Tours, the local rugby club. Here was my ticket to freedom. No more detention in *Stalag 17*, our nickname for the room where you spent weekends if you were punished.

From the beginning I knew cooking was going to be my raison d'être. I went from an average student in high school to a very good cooking school student. Learning comes easily when it makes sense, and it gives you the missing pieces to becoming what you want to be in life. Conversely, when there is no apparent purpose to the learning, it becomes an impossible chore. At the Centre everything came easily except English. Frankly, I was much more interested in looking at my English teacher's legs than studying the language. Why did I need to learn English if I was to become a chef? Only when I came to America did it become apparent why I should have paid attention. In hindsight I wish I had a crystal ball to show me how hard being unable to communicate would be, and how it would make me feel not only ignorant, but downright stupid.

The first internship of my apprenticeship was in Lourdes, the famous city in the Pyrenees where the Virgin Mary appeared to Bernadette Soubirou. Millions come to Lourdes each year for a vision of the Virgin Mary. Sick people come expecting a miracle.

When you are fifteen, you don't have your priorities set properly. I chose Lourdes not for its culinary or cultural opportunities, but because my favorite rugby team played there. I could see and talk to my rugby idols every day! This was a dream come true.

Michel and his brother Jacques at the beach in Lancieux, 1957

39

Jean and Maurice Prat, Rancoule, Jean Barthe, Papillon Lacaze and the Labuzy brothers ... their names may not be household words in America, but they were my superheroes.

There was progress on the culinary front. My internship taught me speed and preparation. The food was good, not fancy, but there was a lot of it and it needed to be produced quickly. I learned organization, and how to work in a small area while keeping it clean. An example is preparing potatoes. In America, there are usually three kinds of potatoes the kitchen prepares – boiled, mashed, and fried. In France, there might be 365 kinds of potato dishes. You can't do that in a sloppy, disorganized kitchen.

My next two internships were in Brittany, at the Hotel Printania in Dinard, only ten kilometers from Ploubalay where I had grown up. This was my stomping ground. I love that part of Brittany for its rocky coast (the Côte d'Armor) and its unpredictable storms and ever-changing weather. (I am not a person who likes consistent weather. Though I live in Florida, I travel to Vermont frequently for my position with New England Culinary

Hotel Printania, summer of 1957

Institute. Plus my wife and I go back to France every year. There is plenty of weather variety in my life.)

The kitchen at the Hotel Printania was fabulous. We had an ocean view, unheard of in professional kitchens. There were restrictions, too, such as the small refrigerator which allowed us to handle only small deliveries. Luckily, we had ready access to abundant seafood.

Hotel Printania was a small hotel with thirty-five rooms, with meals included in the room price: a prix fixe menu, as well as a small á la carte menu. We had fifty to seventy customers and a menu that changed daily. The food was *cuisine bourgeoise*, a very rich cuisine featuring local ingredients (*cuisine de terroir*).

Everything was done to perfection. Meals were not served on plates, but rather were presented on silver trays. After the wait staff served the customer, the tray was returned to the kitchen to be reset. After a short while the customer was offered the entire tray, for a second time.

I began to master cooking methods for preparing certain foods like Dover Sole. We served Dover Sole *Meunière* twice a week. The fish came from small boats that went out to the Channel. The fish were utterly fresh, never iced. The fishermen brought the catch each morning, insisting on cash payment.

When you cook fifty to sixty sole to order on a charcoal stove, practice makes it perfect. Few people know this, but you must put a thin slice of potato under the tail of the Dover Sole so that the tail will not burn. It has to be cooked evenly. We finished it with a perfect *beurre noisette*, a hazelnut butter. You "hear" when it is perfect when the drizzling in the pan stops. This means the water has evaporated. At that point, add the lemon juice. *Voila!* Perfect Dover Sole.

I made omelets once a week. An omelet is often regarded as an undistinguished dish, but making them correctly is an art. Omelet making is, at once, simple and difficult, the challenge being in customizing to individual taste, which requires various preparations. Some people like omelets well-done, others just-done, and others almost liquid, which we call *baveuse* in French. The eggs are beaten, seasoned, and poured into a hot omelet pan in which butter has been stirred briskly with a fork

Michel and friends in Tours, 1955

to insure the whole pan is heated evenly. The garnish should be done before rolling the omelet. The whole process must be done rapidly.

The perfect omelet is a cross between a pregnant lady and a cigar – because it should be oblong, slightly plump – and should have no color and no wrinkles. Making omelet after omelet is how I learned. With each one you make a tiny adjustment, a small course adjustment, the temperature of the pan, the amount of butter, the whisking of the eggs. Finally, perfection is achieved. There are no words to describe the process. You just need to make a thousand omelets. (Years later, when I was making omelets to be photographed for a magazine, I had to make seven before I made what I considered to be the perfect one!)

Chef Yvon demanded perfection. When we were at the omelet station, the reward – if you lived up to his standard – was that you could leave after service, and didn't have to clean up the kitchen. This badge of honor was worth seeking. Chef Yvon was a small man and probably an alcoholic, but he taught me how to make *beurre blanc*, which means "white butter." If you ever want to start an argument between two chefs, ask them how they make beurre blanc. Chefs have very strong opinions about this.

Internships were three months without a day off. Now I know why France turned into a thirty-five-hour work week. I avoided Chef Yvon in the kitchen and spent time thinking of pranks. There was a first-year apprentice in the kitchen nicknamed The Petit Michel. He annoyed me by constantly asking what I was doing. One day I sliced a cork and put it in a bowl and told him the chef wanted him to pound it until he could smell the garlic. He pounded that cork for over an hour, and there was cork all over the kitchen. Chef Yvon asked me what he was doing and slapped me hard for my prank.

The real reason I spent two summers in Dinard was the waitresses. They were good-looking and had a good sense of humor, a necessary ingredient in an otherwise stressful environment. Sometimes we had no break all day and had to clean fish while the waitresses had to polish the silver in the afternoon.

Chef Yvon was a short, middle-aged man with a big nose. His face was red, and he had bandaids on his fingers from self-inflicted cuts. His toque was very tall, to compensate for his shortness. Chef Yvon was jealous of my good relations with the waitresses, and he would make extra work to keep me from going to the beach in the afternoon to meet up with my friends, especially my favorite waitress. One day this ornery man put the *rondeau* – the copper pots – on the fire to turn

Jacqueline, Hotel Printania, summer of 1957

43

them black so that I would have to spend my break cleaning them. But when you want to meet a girl on the beach, you become very, very creative.

I consulted with Monsieur Planchon, who was the pot washer. He was about seventy-five and quite a guy. He had all his teeth and had never been to the dentist, and would chew off the good porcelain from plates just to show off how strong his teeth were. We interns found this pretty amusing. In France your greatest fear is that you go through all the work to become a chef only to become a seventy-five-year-old pot washer. He also had a secret recipe for a mixture for cleaning pots, and he gave me his secret recipe–coarse salt, vinegar, egg white, and sand. "Sand?" I asked him. "Where do you think I can get sand?" And he replied, "At the beach!" So I took my pots to the beach and spent my break cleaning the pots with my friend, Yvette. By the time we were finished, the pots were so clean they glowed.

Les Halles, 1957

Off to Paris

Finally, I got bored and wanted change. I got tired of the chef-tyrant and decided to move to Paris. I had been having fun with the girls in Dinard, but I was going nowhere professionally, and the only kind of comment I received from the chef was, "You should try plumbing, you will never become a chef." When I went to say goodbye to Chef Yvon, he told me "Not bad, little one." I was stunned.

"Excuse me, Chef, what did you say?" He replied, "Well, I mean you are not bad. There's a couple of things you can do to improve." For someone who had been mentally and physically abused for two years without a compliment, I interpreted the chef's comments as, "You are a goddamn genius, you are a superstar." And it instantly went to my head.

In the 1950s, if you were a cook and didn't work in Paris you had no credibility. All the best restaurants were in Paris. I remember a friend asking, "Do you work in Paris?" I answered "no" and returned the question. He said, "No, I do not either, but I have a friend working there!" I became fixated on the idea of working in Paris, the place to work.

I was an eighteen-year-old country bumpkin, overwhelmed by the City of Light. First, I had to find a room. An apartment was out of the question. It took two weeks to find a place. Meanwhile I stayed at a friend's, only a block from the Champs Elysées. My room was a *chambre de bonne*, a maid's room, on the eighth floor, with the bathroom at the end of the hall. Later, I found a room in what is now one of the most beautiful neighborhoods in Paris, near Place des Voges, called Rue des Tournelles, near La Bastille. Then, it was a tough neighborhood, but with a great dance hall, called *Le Balajo*.

It was 1957. I was on my own with a little bit of talent and almost no self-assurance. I joined L'Association des Cuisiniers de Paris – a cooks' association that can be helpful in finding jobs.

I did not want a full-time job, because I wanted to explore and find a situation to improve my culinary skills. I had few connections of my own – very important in the kitchen trade – so I started to work as an extra, or what might be called a "temp" today. L'Association sent you to a restaurant to fill a position for someone who was sick or just did not show up. An advantage of being an extra was that you got paid cash and were given a subway ticket. I liked that. Especially the word cash! My first day as an extra was at a brasserie (a large bistro) near Le Metro, La Motte Picquet. It was required to have your own uniform and knives. You were provided an apron.

The chef showed me my station, showed me the *mise en place* (which means you have all your ingredients cut and ready to be cooked), and immediately I told him, "Chef, this is not the way it should be done." Guess what? He kicked me out. At 9:00 in the morning I went next door and sat on the terrace, ordered a café crème and a croissant, and read *L'Equipe*, a daily newspaper that covers sports. That afternoon I went to Jardin des Plantes, the park where the English nannies were babysitting little kids from rich families. The nannies wanted to learn French, and I wanted to learn how to speak English. This was a convenient coincidence, and it sure beat mopping the floor in a kitchen! However, I found it hard to concentrate on learning English with all the pretty nannies in the park.

I got fired eight times in seven days because I was such a know-it-all! Finally, it did sink into my head that if I had to make money and learn, maybe I should shut up. The following week, the placement director from the association called me and asked me why I could not keep a job. "Well, sir, I have not found the right job yet." He said, "Okay! You better stay where I'm going to send you today." He sent me to a brasserie called Chez Jenny, on the Boulevard du Temple and Metro Republique. When I walked in the kitchen and handed my employment slip to the chef, my life changed. I had learned a critical lesson in the culinary world – to follow the chef's orders without complaint or argument. You know the bumper sticker, "Question Authority." Not with the chef!

Welcome to the Real World

Chef Bernard stood about 6'6" and was built like a linebacker. He looked down at me, made eye contact, and calmly said, "I bet that you are a smart ass," to which I replied, "No, not me, sir." He was a foot taller, but I detected in him something rare – a very kind man, who was gentle, calm, but firm. I knew I was going to be happy there.

He realized in me that he had a wild horse. If he could break me, he would have a solid cook. Not a chef. The word chef was not used then like it is now. You had to earn the title, and it took many years. It took me twenty-five. (I am a slow learner.)

Chef Bernard asked me to do two things in front of him. One was to chop an onion, and two was to make an omelet. This may sound ridiculous, but he wanted to see my knife skills and to see if I was a good technician by making a perfect omelet the first time. If so, he would know if he could teach me something.

Chez Jenny was one of the most popular *brasseries Alsaciennes* in Paris. The Alsatian food was heavily influenced by the proximity of Alsace province to Germany. Menu items included sauerkraut, paté, smoked meats, and lots of pork, all heavy food. I remember *Longe de Veau au Riesling avec Spatzel* – braised veal. And when the chef says braise, it better not be boiled. When you braise, first brown the food in hot fat, then cover and cook slowly in a small amount of liquid over low heat. Chef Bernard was a stickler for the basics in cooking. Every time cold food went out of the kitchen, it was on a cold plate, and hot food on a hot plate.

We were fourteen in his kitchen brigade. The brigade is a system of shuffling a kitchen so that each worker is assigned a set of specific tasks. These tasks are often related by cooking method, equipment, or the type of foods being produced. The chef is *le gros bonnet* which means the big hat. There was no such thing as the title of executive chef in those days.

The sous chef is the second in charge in the kitchen and becomes the chef when he is absent. The *chef de partie* is the station chef. This person produces menu items and specials under the direct supervision of the chef or sous chef. There are different chefs de parties for the different stations, for example, one can be a *chef de partie saucier*.

The *commis* works under the chef de partie. The first commis usually has two to three years' experience after apprenticeship. The second commis is just out of apprenticeship, a rookie in the cooking world. He does a lot of mis en place work. There is a joke about the third commis, sometimes referred to as *aux epinard*, meaning you still have to clean the spinach in the kitchen and are not moving up the ladder very quickly.

The *saucier*, responsible for all sautéed items and most sauces, holds one of the most demanding jobs in the kitchen. The *charcutiers* make sausage, paté, and terrine, ham, bacon, cured meat, all the trimmings for the *choucroute* (sauerkraut.)

In our brigade we had one pastry chef, Tony, a senile patissier who made only one thing, plum tarts. The *quetsch* tart is made with purple plums, and *mirabelle* is made with yellow plums. Tony made two hundred a day.

The dishwashers were always from Algeria, runaways from the Algerian War. Algeria was a French colony until 1962 and was fighting for its independence. Defectors needed jobs and took menial work like dishwashing that the French didn't want. It's not different in American kitchens today, only the languages change.

French Muslims were five percent of the overall population when I left France in 1964. Now it is ten percent. *Steak frite* was the national dish then, a dish that both rich and poor liked. Now it is couscous, because of the strong Algerian and North African influences of immigrants to Paris. (Similar changes in national cuisine had occurred after the French Vietnam war ended in 1954.)

Amadou, a native Algerian, was the dishwasher's boss, and Chef Bernard's right hand. Notable about Chef Bernard's kitchen was that this was the first time in my life I could work without fear of being slapped, kicked on the ankle, or reprimanded in front of my peers.

Sauerkraut was popular because the Alsatians had a strong influence in the food service business in Paris, and it was a staple in their native land. We sold one ton of sauerkraut a day in the brasserie. One ton! And everything was made on the premises. There were at least ten ways to serve it – from simple sauerkraut with frankfurters and boiled potatoes to the *Jenny Speciale*, served on a silver platter. You start the Jenny Speciale by placing half a bottle of champagne in the middle of the tray, then arrange the sauerkraut, the bacon, the smoked pork, and three kinds of sausage. The sauerkraut was heated on a burner, also on the tray, and doused with champagne. This was the first time I understood about the interrelation of sweetness, sourness, and fat. The chemistry of taste is what fine cooking is all about.

The brigade at Chez Jenny was comprised of some serious characters, most of them heavy drinkers. Every morning I had my café crème and croissant at Le Tenin, a bar next door to Chez Jenny, often with my friend Serge, the chef de partie, and Zeppe, the sous chef. As soon as the bartender saw them, he made two double espressos and double rums. For breakfast. If either one didn't show up at the usual time at Le Tenin, the other polished off the first round. Then, when the late-comer arrived, they had another double round. Try going to work at 8 A.M. with two or three double rums under your belt. For Serge and Zeppe there was nothing to it.

Another character was Rolland. He and Serge were Vietnam veterans, called *ancien d'Indochine*. They claimed that they contracted yellow fever while in Vietnam, and blamed this for their heavy drinking. We called them *tête brulée*, hot heads. They were undeniably tough guys.

Because of the environment Chef Bernard kept a close and protective eye on me. Perhaps I was the son he never had. He was like a father, but unlike my own. He was strict, but scrupulously fair. He knew when the brigade was stressed and started joking around to lighten things up. I have adopted this same technique to break tension in the kitchens I have managed.

Occasionally he took a potato and knocked down one of our toques (the tall, traditional paper hats of kitchen professionals.

The tradition has been diluted today by kitchen staff wearing different hats to denote individual specialties, and now most French chefs do not wear a hat at all. Many American chefs wear a baseball cap in the kitchen! The practical purpose of hats is to keep hair out of the food.)

One day Chef Bernard knocked down Serge's toque. Serge was working as *garde-manger*, who is responsible for cold food preparation, such as salads and dressings, also cold appetizers, patés, etc. The garde-manger also supervises the butcher. Serge retaliated and threw a potato at the chef, surprising him. He took off after Serge, chasing him around the kitchen. Serge, a former paratrooper, jumped through the window into a pile of sand in the courtyard. A couple of weeks later, the scenario was repeated, but the chef had replaced the pile of sand with a couple of kegs of beer, concealed by a thin layer of sand. It wasn't pretty when Serge landed on the kegs of beer!

The kitchen is a chef's kingdom. The rule is, if you are not a cook, you need to call to the chef for permission to *enter* his kingdom. A certain English waiter, Peter, had the bad habit of entering through the kitchen without the chef's permission. Chef Bernard warned him by throwing heavy copper pots into Peter's legs and saying, "Watch out! You're going to get hurt in this kitchen, Peter."

To which Peter replied, "Yeah, yeah, yeah, Chef, don't worry about it."

There is a hierarchy in the kitchen, and *politesse*, or rules of behavior. One night I was on the garde-manger station doing the graveyard shift. There were two or three of us. We started the shift at 8:00 P.M., but at the end of the service around 11:00, we took over all the stations until closing, then put everything away and cleaned the kitchen, closing the place around 4:00 A.M. In those days there was sawdust on the kitchen floor. If you spilled something, it was absorbed by the sawdust and swept out at the end of the day.

It became very busy around midnight after the shows were over. The restaurant was within walking distance from Le Cirque d'Hiver, a permanent circus. At this time the movie, *Trapeze*, starring Burt Lancaster, Tony Curtis, and Gina Lollabrigida was being filmed there. The entire cast came for dinner and sat in Peter's station. He was very excited and barged into the kitchen with a special order but, again, forgot to ask chef's permission. The special order was for the garde-manger, my station. Peter ignored me and went directly to Chef Bernard, who moved slowly out of his office and told Peter that this was his lucky night, and he personally would take care of the order.

Peter followed the chef. Suddenly Chef Bernard turned around, grabbed Peter under the arms, lifted him off the ground and sat him on the stove. Calmly, the chef said, "I told you one day you will get hurt." Peter's pants started to catch on fire. He ran out of the kitchen by the back door, pants on fire, never to return. This was the consequence of ignoring the kitchen protocol. Chef Bernard handled the order as if nothing had happened. Luckily, people did not think in terms of law-suits in those days. I doubt Peter ever mentioned the incident to anyone.

Chef Bernard wanted everyone to sit down for a one-hour lunch and dinner. The meals took place even if you were late or your mise en place was not done. Amadou set up the table and sat next to the chef. The chefs de partie had tablecloths and silver tableware, and bottled water and wine. For us, the com-mis, it was Chinese style, meaning no tablecloths, and a pile of plates with stainless steel tableware on the top. The food, however, was the same for all. No one would start eating until the chef began. This tradition motivated the commis to work hard to climb the ladder to sit at the table with tablecloths.

Newcomers learned fast to sit at the last seat at the table, and if the chef had a guest, to eat standing up. As you were promoted, you moved up towards the head of the table with its white table cloth, wine, and water. When I started, I was second *commis saucier*. In one year I was promoted to first commis. I never made chef de partie, but I became *tournant*, the "relief" person in the kitchen, similar to a relief pitcher in baseball, but more difficult. Imagine if Mariano Rivera, the Yankee's star reliever, had to also play catcher, first base, short-stop, and outfield. I may have moved up, but I don't remember getting a raise.

Chef Bernard never took a kickback from the purveyors, probably the only chef in Paris not to do so. He used his connections another way, for the benefit of the brigade. On the last day of every month, he rewarded the entire brigade by taking us all to *Les Halles*, Paris's famous marketplace which unfortunately no longer exists. It was a swell place. In addition to housing the wholesale food business, there were hundreds of restaurants. Emile Zola, the famous French author who wrote about the working people, called it "The Belly of Paris."

What was once Les Halles has now moved to the outskirts of Paris, near the Orly Airport, and is known as *Rungis*. It is bigger, better, more convenient, and has state of the art refrigeration. However, I still miss Les Halles with its symphony of sounds and smells and never-ending supply of memorable characters. Truly, it was an unforgettable slice of life.

Chef Bernard brought us to one of the bistros at Les Halles, where we could eat and drink whatever we wanted. Chef Bernard then signed the check and gave it to one of the purveyors, making it their treat. Chef Bernard didn't care how much we had to drink or eat, but we better be in top shape at 8:00 A.M. the following day.

Les Halles was my personal kingdom. I came to know a lot of people by sight, and vice versa. Sometimes one of the purveyors gave me a piece of fruit to taste, asking, "What do you think about this, little one?" Most of the restaurants in Les Halles were simple bistros, intermingled with elegant places like Le Pied de Cochon, where the chic came for a late dinner after the theater. Details flood back to me even now, like the vendor at Rue des Lombards and Boulevard Sebasteaupol who made the best French fries I have ever eaten. They were served in a *cornet*, a cone made of newspaper. The rumor was they were cooked in horse grease! I ate them with vinegar, washed down by beer.

The streets were narrow, and the gendarmes controlled the traffic, because they had to control the truck drivers, who had very short fuses, too. There was so much activity there that if you had an aerial view, it would appear to be a city of ants. What I loved most about the market was the camaraderie among the purveyors. It was a magical scene, lit by open fires, that came to life only at night. Les Halles was open from 2:00 A.M. until 8:00 A.M., because the restaurant people who came needed everything before the next day began. Despite the chaos, there was no crime. The huge stacks of fruits and vegetables, the hanging meat, the fish on ice, the truck drivers, the prostitutes, a special mix of chestnuts that were roasted in the fall ... all blend together to create an unforgettable tapestry united by food.

One reason Chef Bernard took us to Les Halles was to observe the *Les forts des Halles* which means "the strong guys." They wore long white blouses, actually buttonless coats, that were pulled over the head. They carried sides of beef and other produce by hand or by cart. A typical breakfast for them might consist of onion soup, pigs' feet, paté, and bread, washed down by a bottle of red wine. No worries about cholesterol here. They worked like devils.

Three or four nights a week I took the long way home in order to go through Les Halles. Instead of going directly along Republique to La Bastille, I walked down Porte Saint Martin, then Rue St. Denis. I watched the buyers, as they checked the produce, fish, and meat. I observed how they were buying, how they checked for quality. I was picking up the tricks of the trade, tricks I later passed to those whom I taught in the kitchen, especially the students at New England Culinary Institute.

When buying, first and foremost, your first task is to earn the respect of the purveyor. For example, when you buy a case of oranges, you always have to turn the box upside down to open it to make sure none of the blemishes are actually frozen spots. Then, if you buy an eighty count, you have to count them to make sure. The purveyors do not like to see you do this, but it shows you know what's going on.

Dishonest purveyors will barter for lunch or dinner with pilfered items from their own stock. Here's how it works: the purveyor stops at a favorite restaurant where the chef gives his order, for example six eggplants, six lemons, twelve tomatoes, twenty-four oranges, and so forth. He opens one box and takes an orange, then opens a second box, takes another, and so forth. Who is going to miss one orange? If you do not count each box in your order, you will be paying for the purveyor's free lunch.

The purveyor's boss is well aware of this practice, but closes his eyes or looks the other way. My thinking is very simple. I tell my students, "When you go to buy a car, it has four hub caps in the showroom. If you came to pick up the car, there are only three hubcaps, you'd be upset, wouldn't you?"

Purveyors respect buyers who check, and if they respect you, they also will tell you, *Chef, this is not for you*, and bring you around back, where the fresh produce has just arrived. Mutual respect is everything. If you are not happy with merchandise, return it. No questions asked. If you accept bad merchandise and do not count, you are a marked man.

Several nights a week on my own way home I'd go to Avenue de Rivoli to La Bastille. If I had money I took a cab, because the subways were not running at that late hour. (Subways start running at 5:00 or 5:30 in the morning.) Le Balajo was a dance hall where waiters, waitresses, cooks, cab drivers, and tourists hung out. It was packed at 5:00 A.M. Lots of girls went there to get picked up – that was our perspective ... I am sure the girls had another. We danced until 7:00. Afterwards, I went to my favorite bistro, the Dupont, for hot chocolate and then home to bed. This was my life in Paris.

I started clicking in business. Not only had I improved my speed and skills, but I began understanding the big picture of how things worked and what you needed to do to be successful. I was a country bumpkin working in a sophisticated restaurant in Paris, the City of Lights. I owe everything to Chef Bernard. I drank in what he was teaching, no matter how difficult. I flourished from the attention of a man who was firm but had a big heart. Not only did he teach me in the kitchen, he taught me in Les Halles. I will never forget him, and my teaching pays tribute every day to Chef Bernard.

My Years in the Navy

I was drafted in September 1958 at nineteen and chose to go into the Navy, hoping this would help keep me out of the war in Algeria. I spent two months in stupid, basic training in Hourtin, near Bordeaux, but I did learn how to iron my clothes properly and how to fold my clothes all the same size so they could fit in my bag. It was the first time I slept in a hammock and found it quite comfortable. After two months I went to boot camp and learned how to clean a rifle blindfolded. We were all in top physical shape. At boot camp they trained us, mentally and physically, to get ready for the Algerian War. Training included a 10k run in boots, not sneakers, push ups, sit ups, night training, and climbing walls. Boot camp was *le parcour du combatant* to prepare us for combat.

I got lucky and was not sent to Algeria, but assigned as the cook on a tugboat in the high seas. *Le Mamouth* was harbored in Cherbourg and was probably the oldest ship of the French

Le Mamouth, 1959

Navy, still powered by coal. There were forty in the crew, plus two dogs. Most of us had been drafted, and most of us were from Brittany or Normandy. I was the only one who was not a fisherman and fearless on the water. Our duty was to rescue anyone in trouble, whether from a sailboat or a tanker.

I learned quickly what the crew liked to eat. Most of the fishermen were good cooks, as good as I was. We were not your typical Navy. Not one of us had an official uniform. We were free-spirited pirates, loading coal and working hard in the high seas, always enjoying a joke. The military police never gave us problems if we were caught in a barroom brawl onshore. They protected us, because they knew we were responsible while at sea, and we had dangerous missions.

When "on alert," you might be called to rescue someone at any time. Painting filled the time between hair-raising rescues. There was always painting to fill the time. We used to say *peinture sur merde – égal propreté*, which translates to "paint over shit and it will be clean." With a lot of time to kill, you painted and then painted some more!

Every month we received fifteen francs, which is about $3, ten stamps to write to our parents, and seventeen packs of cigarettes. I never figured out why seventeen. Why not fifteen or twenty? I did not smoke and used my cigarettes to play poker, the second most popular pastime after painting. I bet a different number of cigarettes for each hand. The poker games could go on for days. I had fun learning, but I ran out of cigarettes after two or three days, because I was a lousy bluffer.

After one year I asked to be transferred to Brest, because I got seasick in bad weather and that was not fun. Not wanting to let down my shipmates, I had tried to hide it. But seasickness is not something you can hide!

Working for the Admiral in Brest

To my delight I was transferred to be cook for Admiral Jubelin, a four-star admiral in Brest. He lived at a place called "Le Chateau." The pastry chef was a Basque named Toyos, and Jeannot was the chauffeur. A maitre d' served the admiral, his young wife and two children.

The admiral was not a *fayot*, meaning not your typical military man. He was well-read and well-rounded. He did not like formal receptions and kept them to a minimum. This meant that we had to feed the family, drive the kids to school, and do the shopping. The admiral liked to have breakfast with us in the kitchen, read the paper, and talk about soccer.

Admiral Jubelin had two passions. The first was bird

hunting, and the second was *petanque*. Petanque is the ultimate game, even though it is quite simple. You draw a circle 35 centimeters in diameter, and from there you throw what is called the *cochonet* or little ball. Literally it means "the little pig," and you throw it between six and ten meters. Next, throw your *boule* (the larger ball), and the one who comes closest to the little pig wins. Some are *placeur*, and some are *tireur*. The placeur is the one who throws the ball first, as close as possible to the little pig. The tireur has the intention of shooting his ball and trying to kick your ball out. Usually, you play in pairs, with three boules. The first one to reach thirteen points is the winner. You can play anywhere, so long as there is a dirt or rock surface. The admiral had a court built for us. So we played petanque with the admiral, and in the fall he even took some of us bird hunting with him.

Throughout my life, I have played petanque in Paris, Vermont, and now in Florida. In Florida there are the players from France, Canada, and of course America. There are women, and the age range is very wide, from young to old. It is still a sport I love and look forward to playing whenever I have the opportunity.

I really enjoyed my job as chef to Admiral Jubelin, but unfortunately we were only getting Navy pay, fifteen francs. Jeannot, the chauffer, and I often were broke, about three times a month, but still had the urge for entertainment. Every Saturday we read *Le Telegramme*, the local newspaper, about the local weddings. We memorized the names of the bride and groom. You can see where this is heading. At that time the average wedding had two hundred guests. We asked the admiral to borrow the car, and he never refused. He did request us not to display the four star flag, signaling the admiral was on board. We never did, but we sure thought about it!

So we crashed the weddings and drank and danced and had a fabulous time, free of charge. Every so often people looked at us with some suspicion or surprise, so we told them we worked for the shipyard where at least a quarter of the population in town was employed.

I moonlighted at a cooking job in town to make ends meet.

The chef was Swiss, and he had a daughter, Rollande, who later became my girlfriend. Her mother, Madame Gabou, never made business transactions without consulting a psychic. She wanted to know if Rollande and I had a future together. I was not interested in getting married at that time. Madame Gabou paid for my consultation with Madame Petitbon in a dark apartment located on Rue de Siam. Entering the room, on the wall above the chimney, I saw a lot of thank-you letters for her good advice. This was in 1960. She told me that my father would die quickly. He died six months later of cancer. She told me I would meet my wife, who was taking care of sick people near the water while I was listening to music. Two years later I met my wife, a nurse, while dancing on a boat. She also told me that we would cross a large ocean to go to a country where there were problems with black people. We came to the U.S. in 1964, in the middle of the civil rights protests and violence.

Obviously the mention of meeting my wife of the future meant that my alliance with Madame Gabou's daughter was not to be long!

A friend being discharged

Chicken Gumbo

Serves 4

Prep time : 45 minutes

Cooking Time : 45 minutes

The Story

Talking about gumbo in Louisiana is like talking beurre blanc with French chefs: everybody has the best recipe, of course. In gumbo what makes the difference is the roux and how it is cooked, which gives this unique taste. Try this one.

The Recipe

½ lb butter or chicken fat
½ lb flour
6 slices bacon, diced
1 large onion, diced ¼"
2 green peppers, diced ¼"
2 red peppers, diced ¼"
3 C crushed tomatos (canned)
3 qt chicken stock
1 2½ to 3 lb whole chicken
Salt
1 pkg sliced okra, frozen
1 lb links andouille or spicy sausage (chorizo)
2 Tbsp gumbo file
5 cloves garlic, chopped
Cayenne to taste

Melt the butter or chicken fat in a cast-iron pan, add flour, and mix well. Place in a 400° oven. Cook stirring frequently until the roux has a brick color, it should have a nutty smell. Remove from the oven. In a large heavy-gauge pot, sauté bacon; add the onions and peppers, cook slowly until tender. Add brown roux, crushed tomato, chicken stock, whole chicken and salt. Cook until the chicken is tender. Remove and pick the meat off the bone and dice. Add okra and andouille, cook 15 minutes. Remove andouille and slice, return to the pot with the picked chicken. Add gumbo, garlic, and cayenne.

Taste. Season. Taste.

This should be served with a bowl of boiled rice.

Running with the Big Dogs

I had escaped the war in Algeria and was actually having a fun time. I was honorably discharged on January 11, 1961, and returned to Paris, which I had missed badly.

I went to La Grille, a street with many bars where cooks gather every Wednesday. This was where you found out about good jobs, not in the newspaper. A friend told me there was an opening at Lucas Carton, located in Place de la Madeleine. It was a two-star Michelin restaurant, one of the best in Paris. I hesitated because I knew the chef, Mark Soustelle, was a bastard, but this was a rare opportunity to work and to learn in one of the best restaurants in Paris. Chef Soustelle had worked with the legendary Escoffier at the Savoy Hotel in London.

George Auguste Escoffier, born in 1846, made invaluable contributions to the world of cooking and single-handedly elevated the status of chefs. He is noted for creating the á la carte menu and strictly enforcing a no drinking rule in the kitchen, which made the environment much more professional. He wrote the book, *Le Guide Culinaire*, still used by cooks, chefs, and culinary students. Escoffier personally created the system of the kitchen brigade, also known as chefs de parties. He also believed in simplifying menus.

I went that afternoon to Lucas Carton to introduce myself and was told to start the following day at 8:00 A.M. I did not sleep that night and was so nervous, I had a small asthma attack the next morning in the metro. I arrived a half hour early to meet the other cooks and get the scoop on what I would be doing. I would be *entremetier,* the station where all the vegetables and garnishes for the roasts, poultry, fish, and soups are prepared.

Now twenty-two, I was at the bottom of the ladder again. There were only two of us in the station, the chef de partie and me. His name was Roger, and he was from Alsace. He quickly gave me my list for mise en place. You could cut the pressure with a knife. The chef did not show up until 10:00 A.M. He had been at the market. We had to do an unbelievable mise en place with five soups for starters. Talk about perfection – *brunoise*, julienne, medium dice, *tournée* vegetables for *petite marmite*. (Petite marmite is a chicken broth cooked ahead of time and served in the same small ceramic pot in which it is cooked. Tournée is a cut shaped like an oblong, seven-sided little football. As you can imagine, this takes a great deal of skill.)

I began shaking like a leaf when the chef entered the kitchen. Of course, he came right to my station, plunged his hand into my bowl of diced potatoes and rolled them on the table like small dice to see if they were uniform. He picked out two or three which were not perfect, and he looked at me and told me to start over again. I did not know whether to cry or quit, but I did not want to give him the satisfaction of seeing me cry. No crying in the kitchen! I was proud of the job I had done, but it was not good enough for Chef Soustelle. He demanded perfection – if, indeed, there is such a thing in cooking. Braised lettuce, absolutely the same length. Small stuffed cabbage strictly the same size.

We also made *tomato au torchon*. The procedure is: peel and seed a tomato, wrap it in a towel, squeeze the juice out, then twist into a ball shape. They all must be uniform! Even though I was the entremetier, my duties included making *le petit pot de chocolat*. The recipe was on the wall, and it was a simple recipe, or so I thought. Mix eggs and sugar, but in a very particular way! Of course, I learned the hard way.

The first time I made le petit pot de chocolat, Chef Soustelle corrected me very quickly. The eggs and the sugar must be mixed with a wooden spoon, not over-mixed, and not under-mixed. If you mix with a whisk, you incorporate air. Bubbles are to be avoided. When the milk is added, slowly stir with a wooden spoon, adding the melted chocolate. The mixture is poured into a petit pot. Then, take an oven-proof container, line with a towel, place the petit pot on top of the towel, fill the pan with cold water, and place in the oven. (Remember, at that time we cooked with coal and had no thermostat.)

Le petit pot de chocolate is a chocolate version of *crème*

caramel. One day I had single bubble on top of my petit pot de chocolat, and I heard about it for the next week from Monsieur Soustelle. He said, "You should try grave digging; you're good for nothing. If idiocy was a glass cage, you would break the cage to get in!"

The chef was not a great teacher. Learning is much harder if you are in constant fear of screwing up. But I just gritted my teeth, because at least I was learning from the best of the best. Anyone who worked with Monsieur Soustelle will ask, "How many perfect *pommes soufflés* can you make out of ten?" I thought I was pretty good, because I could make six.

Here's how to make pomme soufflé. Cut Idaho potatoes into long, perfect rectangles. Slice them with a mandoline (a kitchen utensil for cutting thin slices), dip the slices into cold water, and remove immediately to avoid oxidation. Fry in a 250° oil. If you are lucky, the potato will puff, but this takes practice, and there are so many variables. If the potato has too much starch, it turns to sugar and browns too quickly. Monsieur Soustelle could make ten slices like magic out of one potato time after time. This was the only time I saw him smile!

Although Chef Soustelle was not a good teacher, I really learned how to cook in his kitchen, because of the constant demand for perfection. When he addressed you, he never let you look directly at him. "Look at my feet," he would order, always trying to humiliate. This was the tradition. Chefs acted as tyrants, and those who were trained in that way passed along the tradition to those trained under them. The goal was absolute authority for the chef in the kitchen.

Even though I had some bad times (really bad times) working there, I hung on for the overall value of the experience. We had a charcoal stove in the center of the kitchen. There was no thermostat in the oven, so to check the temperature you put your hand in the oven. I can still do this and be accurate to within ten degrees.

This was 1960. I really started to learn how to cook. After two years at Lucas Carton, I decided it was time to go back to Brittany. I had done all the stations (except pastry) two or three times and needed a change of pace. I was burnt out from the pressure cooker and humiliation. I needed the Brittany beach and smell of the ocean.

Once I was strolling an Avenue and sat on the bench to read *L'equipe,* the sport newspaper. Sitting next to me was a mother helping her son doing his school homework, but he didn't seem to be very happy doing it at this time. Then a young apprentice Patissier-Boulanger walked by, impeccably dressed, ironed checkered pants, ironed white jacket, carrying a wicker basket with a freshly baked baguette, croissants, and petit pain au chocolat. The woman pointed at him and said to her son, "See, if you don't work well in school you will be like this young man." I was completely devastated.

Sautéed Apple with Cranberry Sherbet
Serves 4

Prep time: 10 minutes

Cooking time: 15 minutes

The Recipe

4 large Golden Delicious apples

1/3 stick butter

½ C granulated sugar

½ C hard cider

½ C heavy cream

2 Tbsp Apple Jack/Calvados

4 scoops cranberry sherbet

Peel, seed, and cut each apple in eighths. In a large frying pan melt the butter, add the sugar, and bring to a light caramel stirring constantly. Add the apple and cook until tender, add the cider and heavy cream, cook an additional 3 minutes. Remove the apple and place into individual bowls. Reduce sauce slowly to heavy cream consistency. Add the Apple Jack/Calvados, flambé and pour over the apple, then scoop sherbet on top. Serve immediately.

My First Job as a Chef

After leaving Chef Soustelle, I found a position as chef in a beautiful manor, Manoir du Stang, in the Brittany town of La Forêt Fouesnant . The Manoir was part of a high-class chain of hotels called Relais et Chateaux. The setting was lovely, and we used only the freshest ingredients in the kitchen.

Once or twice a week, after dinner, I drove to Concarneau to watch the fishing boats unload. Each boat had an assigned space to anchor. After the fish were sorted by size and species, they were transported La Crié to be auctioned. The *mareyeurs* were the buyers. It was like watching a Picasso auctioned. One man set the price, and the mareyeurs, just by making small gestures, increased the bid or buy. Now the auction is done electronically, and is no different than the activity of the floor of the New York Stock Exchange. This was where I learned how to buy fish.

After the auction, everyone went for lunch even though it was 2:00 or 3:00 A.M. Sometimes you would see the elderly ladies who sorted the fish there. The ladies drank in onion soup bowls, pretending to blow on the hot soup, but I eventually learned they were drinking wine!

I started working at Manoir du Stang before Easter, and things went quite smoothly. The waitresses wore the traditional local costume. Sometimes I was the only man at the restaurant. We had three gardeners to take care of the grounds and the vegetable garden, and the milk and butter came from the farm.

It was my first position as chef. All of a sudden I had the responsibility of buying, creating the menu, and managing the food costs and schedule. One of my most important accomplishments was that I learned how to cook shellfish from Madame Anna Le Coze, who worked with me in the kitchen and was the wife of a fisherman. She was completely knowledgeable about the local seafood. As a special treat she made a superb fish soup for the employees called *La Cotriade*.

Something special happened that Saturday before Easter. I had a friend, also named Michel, and we frequented a dance hall called La Bigorne, actually a boat anchored in the bay in La Forêt Fouesnant. Michel called and said, "Come on, let's go to La Bigorne and see what's going on. Maybe there are some tourists over there." We were always chasing the skirts. I did not want to go out that night, because I was trying to focus on my work, especially how to do my mise en place, the meats, relishes, sauces, par-cooked items, spices, vegetables, and other components that I would need for the holiday weekend. In France, Easter is a three-day weekend extending through Monday. I was very conscious of what might happen if I was not prepared.

A chef lives and dies by his mise en place. If there is one item that you do not prepare for, it is guaranteed that item will be on the first ticket coming to the kitchen, and you will be playing catch-up the rest of the day.

Around midnight Michel knocked on my window, yelling at me to shower. I agreed to go, but only for one hour. At that time I did not drink alcohol. Not yet, just my Schweppes tonic water. The dance floor was only about ten by ten feet, so there was not much room for dancing, but plenty for flirting and talking. There was not much action there that night. Just as we were ready to leave, I heard a bunch of girls giggling as they came down the steps to the boat.

I saw her at the end of the dance floor, and it was love at first sight. Her name was Anne-Marie, and forty-two years later, we are still together, very unusual in this business. (I admit that she has had to put up with a lot with me. Being the wife of a chef is not easy. Your husband is never home, always working long, crazy hours.) We argued that first night. She was angry, because I did not offer to drive her back home. The reason was very simple: I did not have any gas and there were no stations open that late. The two sisters she was with were drunk, and she had to ride with them, which she did not want to do. While one of them steered, the other shifted. *Incroyable.* We still laugh about it.

She went back to her job as a nurse in Paris until July, and we went out together that whole month. We were married on October 20, 1962. I decided to return to Paris, accompanied by my new wife. I went back to Lucas Carton, and Chef Soustelle, still a bastard, hired me back. (Maybe I was not so bad as he said! And maybe he was not so bad as I say.)

Anne-Marie was an operating room nurse in a suburb near the Orly Airport. She had housing provided to the nurses. Since we got married without an apartment – actually without anything – I had to find a place to live. It was rough, because I could not find a room, never mind an apartment. I had to go over to the nurses' housing and jump over the wall of the property, a private clinic, to sleep with my wife. One day the head nurse caught me in the shower and gave me hell. Imagine that ... just because I came to sleep with my wife. We knew we could not live that life very long.

The following spring it was back to Brittany, where I took a position as chef at L'Hotel des Dunes in Dinard, the same place where I had been an apprentice barman in my first job. Anne-Marie was pregnant, and in June our son, Stephane, was born, premature at six and a half months instead of nine. He was two and a half pounds when he was born in the small hospital nearby. They had no incubator, and the doctor simply said, "He will make it or not." Two days later we brought him home and he slept in a shoe box near the stove. It was very damp in our villa by the sea. The job ended at the end of the summer, because the season had ended.

We found ourselves, again, without a home, but now with an infant son. We had nothing, so we went to Lausanne in Switzerland. We both got jobs at a very expensive private clinic which had a kitchen brigade of fifteen. We left Stephane with Anne-Marie's mother.

The food at the clinic was not what you would think of as "hospital food." There was one floor exclusively for Saudi sheiks. There were usually at least ten Mercedes in the parking lot. The sheiks had their own food flown in from Saudi Arabia. One of their dietary requirements was that they would only eat birds caught by falcons. (I do not know if there is an associated religious belief.)

The clinic provided us with a small kitchen, a bath, a large bedroom, and even parking for my Renault Dauphine, so we thought this was heaven. The kitchen staff were mostly French, Italian, Portuguese and Spanish. They made us feel we were immigrants at the bottom of the working class.

The Swiss mostly run offices and banks and chocolate stores and do not value manual labor. In their eyes we were low-lifes, but this did not stop us from having fun. For instance, I did not have snow tires for the simple reason that I had no money. But that did not stop us from going to Gstaad, the famous ski resort. Sometimes Anne-Marie, the other nurses, cooks and I would race cars, three or four of us, to nearby Lezin for hot chocolate. The last one to arrive had to pay!

One weekend in Gstaad we had some of the Swiss fondue. After eating fondue, the natives usually drank tea. But as the Frenchman, I decided to drink several glasses of the local wine. Around me people were laughing. I soon found out why they drank hot tea, not wine. The cold going into my stomach solidified the cheese, and I had terrible stomach cramps. How I wished I had drunk tea instead!

We became very homesick, especially for our son, Stephane, living with my mother-in-law. The future was not looking bright. Anne-Marie's uncle, who had a trucking company, told us that we should go to America. This struck a chord, because we both wanted good jobs and to find ways to get ahead. My mother-in-law convinced us that we should not bring our nine-month-old son to a new country before we had jobs and a place to live, but to send for him once we got settled.

It was much easier to emigrate to the United States then than now. Another reason to go to the United States was because many families in Brittany had at least one member living there. Anne-Marie also had a schoolmate who offered us a bed when we first got to New York. With all these factors in mind we filled out applications for green cards to come to the United States. More and more we were thinking and talking about America.

There is still the *What if I had not left?* question that greets me every time I return to France. Life has many directions at any time. We chose the path that led away from our homeland. Had we stayed, who knows? Perhaps I would have become one of those complaining state workers who think only about the next vacation.

But here's one thing I do know – I would never have accomplished in France what I have here. There is too much government bureaucracy and regulation, especially about the work week.

Paris, 1960

Sauteéd Chicken Tenders
Shallot Balsamic Reduction
Serves 4

Prep time: 15 minutes

Cooking time: 15 minutes

The Story

This was one of the best sellers at Tubb's until we closed and moved to Main Street to open the Chef's Table. It was a perfect lunch served in a crepe with mixed greens. When I see some customers they ask me to put it back on the menu.

The Recipe

1 Tbsp canola oil

1 lb chicken tenders

Salt

Pepper

6 shallots, diced very fine

1 Tbsp butter

½ C balsamic vinegar

8 oz white mushrooms (white and firm)

Remove the tendon from the tender. Heat a frying pan and add the oil and the chicken tenders, season. Brown the chicken tenders on both sides. Do not overcook; tenders should be soft to the touch. Cut off the mushroom stems, and cut the cap like big match sticks (julienne). Sauté in the same pan you have used to cook the chicken. Set aside. In a frying pan melt butter, then add the balsamic vinegar and shallots, reduce slowly until you have one tablespoon left. Combine the chicken tenders, mushrooms, and shallot reduction.

Taste. Season. Taste.

Serve with your favorite mixed greens.

Landing in America

After the war and Algerian independence French colonists had to leave the country for safety reasons. Many came to Paris. These French colonists were called les Pied Noir, literally meaning black foot, a name given to them by Algerians people because the French could be distinguished from the natives because of their black boots. The Algerian War had just ended, and the French government required housing priority be given to the returning French colonists. As a result, there were no available apartments in Paris. That was the harsh reality.

Anne-Marie and I left France on May 8, 1964. Our plan was to return to France after two years in America to open a restaurant in Brittany, after having learned how to speak and write English. There were many English tourists now coming to Brittany, so being fluent in English would be critical. Also, by becoming bilingual, it was likely that other opportunities might open up. It seemed quite a simple plan.

Brittany was a very poor region at that time. Most of the jobs were in fishing or the Merchant Marines or the Navy, always called La Royale. Bretons have a great reputation for their skills in sailing and nautical matters. Breton sailors are some of the best in the world.

The inland farms have rocky and poor soil, making it a struggle to survive. Average farm families had ten to twelve children, most of whom left the farms to find work. When Bretons arrived by train in Paris, the first stop often was near Montparnasse, where most of them lived. Most of the girls became maids. They were very good maids, because they were such hard workers. Good looking girls could make even better money by going into prostitution in Paris. That is how it was then. Many of the men who came to Paris worked for the railroads, the Metro, and in bistros. Not surprisingly, Bretons were good candidates for emigration to America.

Many came from the Brittany Triangle, delineated by three small towns – Le Faouet, Scaer and Gourin. Gourin is a town which has a Statue of Liberty in its town center, although a much smaller one than the one in New York harbor. It was donated by Air France in testimony to the 11,500 people from the area who emigrated to the US.

Immigrants who returned to Brittany often built large houses to show everyone that they had succeeded in America. They gave the names, such as La Maison Blanche which means The White House. The same is true in America. Big houses are symbols of big success.

It was not as difficult to obtain a green card then. Local economies in Brittany were dependent on the money sent back to families by Bretons living in America. The same is true today; only the nationalities change. Many Mexican families and towns are kept afloat by the money sent back from relatives living and working in America.

In the nearby village of Roudouallec was a man named Jean Fichan, who immigrated to America after the war but only stayed a couple of years before returning. He was called "The Ambassador," because he helped those who wanted to emigrate from France to America with the necessary and extensive paper work. Many were illiterate. He also helped with travel arrangements, whether by boat or by plane. He did get a fee for booking the travel – as any travel agent would – but never charged any other fee to the many Bretons he assisted.

Many Bretons arrived first in Canada, where there were jobs in logging. Others came down through Detroit, then moved east to New York. Many Bretons were working in New York kitchens at this time. Once someone from Brittany became successful in America, word would get out in their home town, and others from the area were inspired to go, their journey made easier by the network and connections.

Five days after leaving France, aboard the ocean liner *France*, we arrived in the United States. The day is etched into my memory, as if I am watching a movie, even now after forty years. As we passed beneath the Verazzano Bridge, at the mouth of the Hudson River, the fog lifted, the sky cleared, and we saw the Statue of Liberty. Having seen it only on post-cards, the sight took my breath away. The astonishing size and beauty were beyond my expectation or imagination. Like millions of immigrants before us, it was an unforgettable first view of America. I did not know then that the Statue of Liberty had been a gift to the United States by the Paris-based Union Franco-Americaine. The sculptors were Frederic August Bartholdi and Alexandre Gustave Eiffel, the designer of the Eiffel Tower.

Ellis Island had been shut down as an immigration processing center in 1954, and we were glad to be spared that experience. At Ellis Island immigrants had been forced to sleep in large crowded rooms with bunk beds placed very close to each other. Mattresses were removed from the frames during the day and fumigated because of the fear of lice. Some immigrants were detained for long periods of time, and Ellis Island came to be known as the Island of Tears because of those who came, but were sent back to their native countries.

Once in the harbor, we waited in line for a long time to disembark the ocean liner. Our French friends who lived in New York had instructed us to walk from the pier to 42nd Street to go to another friend's apartment, but to our surprise, Pierre Nicolas, a friend of Anne-Marie's, who had gone to the same grammar school with her, came to pick us up. We headed to the apartment of Marie-Louise and Daniel Le Floch, both friends of Anne-Marie's, on 47th Street. They, too, had gone to the same grammar school in Brittany and had all been taught by nuns.

As we walked down the streets of New York, it suddenly hit me that we were in a country where we didn't speak the language. I realized that, instead of looking at the teachers' legs in school, I should have learned English. We were tourists in a foreign land, and we had brought everything we owned, including our hopes and dreams. It was bewildering and overwhelming to be in a new country feeling so helpless. I had never imagined the streets would be so dirty and filled with garbage. As we walked over to the West Side, we saw people who were completely down and out, drunks on the steps, and there was a guy throwing a TV out of the window just in front of us.

I was completely disheartened. Looking back, my expectations had been shaped back in my childhood when American GIs during World War II, in their spotless uniforms, were our saviors. I had been told Americans were impeccable dressers who changed shirts three times a day, so I expected everyone in America to look like those GIs. Other expectations came from the Hollywood image of America in the movies – of pristine streets, shining skyscrapers, a land where everyone was successful. What I saw on the streets of New York was the opposite of clean and prosperous.

I was stunned to see women shopping in hair curlers. In France women take great pride in their appearance, no matter where they are going. In Paris, it is the norm to see little old ladies dressed in elegant suits and high heels as they go down the street to get a loaf of bread!

When we got to the Le Floch's apartment, we were taken aback. It was adequate, but barely so, yet they were proudly telling us how well they were doing, compared to what they had left in France. Daniel was making what we considered a fortune as a waiter at La Côte Basque. We assumed their apartment would be more upscale, because when they had visited us in France, they spent a lot of money. We thought they were rich, but they were living in a very simple two-bedroom flat with no frills. Oddly enough, I remember we ate cold cuts for lunch that day.

After our lunch, we strolled through the streets of New York and then went into Central Park, where everything was in bloom. I was struck by the lovely horse chestnut trees. The horse-drawn carriages were out; in French parks we did not see horses and carriages, only baby strollers and bicycles. I also noticed the dog poop, seemingly everywhere. Not to say there is no dog poop in French parks, but mostly it was on the sidewalks, which are hosed down and cleaned regularly. Dogs and people in France stay on the sidewalks. French parks are well maintained with seasonal flower beds. Security guards make sure the parks stay safe and clean. That day, I was comparing Central Park to Les Tuileries, Les Jardins du Luxembourg, Le

Jardin du Palais-Royal, and Le Parc Monceau, probably not fair comparisons. Looking at Anne-Marie, I said, "I don't know what we are doing here."

I was scared. We had been motivated to emigrate for what seemed like good reasons, but I was ill-prepared for such a different country, a strange language and – at that moment – no vision as to how we could fit in. Perhaps nothing could have prepared me; you just have to experience it. In any case I was overwhelmed and utterly depressed.

I believe if we'd had the money, Anne-Marie and I would have turned around and gone back to France that night. This was the cold reality of culture shock. Consciously and unconsciously I was comparing everything in America to France, the unfamiliar with the familiar. Making these comparisons even more unfair were my fears that I had made a terribly wrong choice in coming here without a job, a home, or knowing English.

We spent the afternoon in the park talking about everything and nothing. Marie-Louise told us she had found a third floor apartment for us between 50th and 51st Streets, on 9th Avenue, above a grocery store. The day was very hot and steamy. On the way back we stopped to see the apartment which was small, but quiet, in the back of the building. We signed a lease for one year, because the rent was so low for New York apartments, around $250. That afternoon Daniel told me there was a job opening at La Côte Basque, the very good French restaurant where he worked. The following day I went for an interview and got the job.

That same day Marie-Louise took us downtown to apply for a phone. I was delighted to find out the phone would be installed the next day, compared to France where it would take two months and endless paper work to get a phone. And that was provided that no one had gone on strike. I noticed that the person taking our application was left-handed, but wrote very fast. This grabbed my attention, because it was the first time I ever saw a left-handed writer, as in France everyone is taught to write right-handed. (I am naturally left-handed, and I admit to not having the best handwriting in the world.)

Two days after our rude introduction to the U.S., we moved into our new apartment behind Madison Square Garden. Anne-Marie and I set about cleaning, anxious to make a comfortable home in this new and unfamiliar country. The landlord said he would pay for the paint and wallpaper and told us he had never had tenants who wanted to fix things up. We were surprised that he was so surprised. We purchased wallpaper, cleaning detergent, and linoleum and went to work.

At a secondhand store we bought two chairs and a Formica table. Then we bought a bed and a lamp at Macy's. We were shocked when the question was asked whether we would pay with cash or credit. We had arrived with $2,000 in our pockets and had always paid for everything in cash. The concept of credit was foreign to us. In France, you did not buy things unless you saved up the cash. The way you handled money and purchasing was a source of personal pride. Another alien concept was the laundromat, which did not exist in France. For some time we washed everything in the tub.

I wrote to my parents bragging that after three days in New York I had a job and an apartment, which my own country could not provide. Alas, three days after writing that letter, I was fired at *La Côte Basque* because of the slow season. *Last come, first out* was the policy, and since I was hired last, I was the first to go. The following day I got a job at La Potinière where Pierre Nicolas told me there was an opening because all the workers were going on vacation. I was soon making $200 a week.

It was an extremely popular restaurant, but more popular than good. I was the only one in the kitchen with any formal training. La Potinière served bistro food, including *poussin*, with *Sauce Americaine* (sauce with a lobster base), filet mignon and *paté en croute*.

When I interviewed at La Potinière, I asked the chef, a little man called Mochon, for a steady, year-round job, not just work for the summer. He said, "No, no, no, don't worry about it," and assured me I would stay on permanently.

I was a saucier, and had never used so many truffles in my life! (In fact, never since, either.) There were two basic truffle sauces, one for filet mignon, one for lobster. I was shocked to see they threw out the extra truffles instead of straining them. I had never seen such waste. The menu was classically French. Even though I was in out of place in America, at least I was at home in the kitchen. I can tell you that in French restaurants everywhere, the line is the line, and the service is the service. I had no trouble getting around the kitchen, and all those who were cooking spoke French.

The methods of cooking, however, included short cuts that went against my training. There were new discoveries as well. I had never seen shrimp cocktail before, and this was my intro-duction to ketchup, which I thought was pretty tasty. I had never seen wild rice before, never mind cooked it, and it was the first time I made vichysoisse, a cold potato leek soup. It was originally known as *crème Gauloise*. The name came from the original name for France, *Gaule*, and its inhabitants the *Gaulois* and *Gauloise*.

Onion soup was a big seller, but not done properly. We baked twenty-four onion soup servings in bowls on a sheet pan. If they dried up, we simply added stock. We never car-melized the onions, essential for a good onion soup. Instead we added Black Jack, which is liquid caramel with some beef base. They bought Black Jack by the gallon and even used it to finish off all the brown sauces. MSG (monosodium glutamate) was used in everything. Because of my classical training, these practices were offensive. But this was America in 1964. Call something *French*, and it would sell.

I had to bite my tongue and adapt to these kitchen practic-es. Had I not, I would have been dismissed as a troublemaker. As an immigrant, I repeatedly told myself, *You cannot fail, no matter how hard the adjustment*. There was no other choice.

The Hilton Hotel on the Avenue of Americas was under con-struction. Where the ABC Building now stands, there was a big hole. Every morning at 4 A.M. I went to *La Petite Potinière*, a res-taurant across the street from *La Potinière*, owned by the same people. I made eight hundred crepes for *La Petite Potinière* by 8 A.M. At *La Potinière* we sold crepes with Sauce Americaine, a lobster sauce, a very big seller.

It took three hours to make eight hundred crepes. There were twenty-two crepe pans, and once you started, you couldn't stop for anything. Picture a flat top stove with eleven crepe pans on the back row and eleven crepe pans on the front. It was assembly line work, but tricky, because if you lost your timing, twenty-two crepes, not just one, burned! Talk about pressure. No time even to answer the phone. I worked alone at La Petite Potinière from 4:00 A.M. to 8:00 A.M., just me and the cockroaches. Cockroaches were a fact of life in all New York kitchens at the time. The exterminator sprayed once a week, but the cockroaches always came back.

When finished, I took my 800 crepes across the street, and worked in the main restaurant until four in the afternoon. One day after Labor Day I counted all the cooks in the kitchen at La Potinière and noticed there was one extra one, but I worked my station as usual. The following day Chef Mochon called me over and said, "Well, I am sorry, somebody came back, and I didn't think he was going to come back."

I said, "You know, Chef, you are not an honest man. You lied to me and I do not like liars."

He replied, "I understand, but you can just go look for a job, and you can always come and have dinner with us until you find a job."

I was upset but indicated I might take him up on the dinner invitation.

I went back the following day to pick up my knives, and Chef Mochon asked me, "You want to eat?"

I nodded in the affirmative.

When he asked me what I wanted to eat, I said, in my fractured English, "Give me a steak."

He went into the walk-in, and I followed him there. The walk-in was just like the one in the movie *Rocky*, with huge sides of meat hanging off enormous hooks in the wall. He was standing by a side of beef, and I patted him on the shoulder, and when he turned around, I decked him harder than I had ever decked anyone in my life – an uppercut right on the chin, and he fell. *Boom!* Just like a bag of potatoes, and he was out ice cold. I turned off the light, closed the door, had someone cook me a steak, then ate it. On the way out, I said to the boss, again in my not-so-polished English, "Go pick up your chef over there, he's in the walk-in."

I was a hero to some of the guys in the kitchen for doing that, but I was not proud of what I had done. I was very upset about being lied to, especially with our nine-month-old son, Stephane, due to arrive the next day, accompanied by my brother-in-law. I was hot-blooded and probably a little crazy back then.

There were many adjustments for my wife as we tried to make New York our home. Food was the biggest culture shock – of course – and the one thing my wife wanted to eat was rabbit with braised carrots. With my fractured English, if I had asked for rabbit at a regular grocery store, people would have looked at me like I had come from another planet.

We were living on 9th Avenue between 50th and 51st Streets, the area known as Hell's Kitchen. In 1881 a *New York Times* reporter went to the West 30s with a policeman to find out about a multiple murder and called the tenement around 10th Avenue and 39th Street "Hell's Kitchen," describing the building as "the lowest and filthiest in the city." Later, this entire district became known as Hell's Kitchen. Many immigrants lived here, because it was affordable, so there was a decidedly ethnic flavor to the neighborhood. The majority of immigrants were Italian, who ran most of the stores.

I was confounded by the dirtiness of the streets of the food market. The streets were not swept, even when littered with food. In Paris, the streets in front of restaurants and food markets are swept and hosed throughout the day and evenings. Here the market was a place where guys were hustling to make money. No one had interest in looking professional, as do the merchants in France, or even in Montreal. There people in the market dress in immaculate white jackets, and carry themselves with a formal demeanor. This is just as true today.

Back to my search for the rabbit. There was a great produce market run by Italians, in the 40s, where Port Authority is now, as well as a grocery store called Molinari on 52nd Street and 9th Avenue. I knew Italians ate rabbit, and found one at Molinari.

I still remember the price – $8 – a small fortune for a rabbit no bigger than a small cat!

Several other aspects of food astonished me – the huge steaks and the practice of keeping chickens on ice! In France we did not ice *anything*; everything had to be fresh. Also, I had never seen iceberg lettuce before. Anne-Marie and I tried iceberg lettuce for a couple of days, but found it tasteless. I still do not consider it lettuce.

My most intriguing discovery was Horn & Hardart's, also known as The Automat on Broadway between 46th and 47th Streets. It was an original concept for a restaurant, but sadly none of these types of restaurants remain.

Horn and Hardart's had opened one restaurant in New York and one in Philadelphia in the early 1900s. The dining room was decorated Art Deco style, with lots of chrome and glass, and featured self-serving vending machines offering single portions.

On one side of the room was a wall full of little windows, outlined in shiny chrome, with food items in each window. On the top of the windows was a list of the food and how much each food item in each window cost. You looked through the clean little windows and selected what you wanted, put your money in, opened the door and voila! One chicken pot pie, something I had never eaten before. And some meringue pie, also an unknown, which could not have cost more than two quarters. Behind the windows people were refilling the empty slots in the windows, and the food was being prepared in a visible commissary-like kitchen. All this, and no need to know English. I thought I had died and gone to heaven.

It was the perfect fast food. The large dining room had round tables about four and a half feet high so that you could eat standing up, shoulder to shoulder with the other customers. (There were regular tables as well.) All you needed was a pocket full of quarters.

Another culture shock was wine. Except for French wine, which we could not afford, the only wine available was mediocre California wine in a jug. In France, good table wine is affordable. One of the most popular wines at this time in America was Mateus, a sweet, fizzy Portuguese wine.

And then there was the beer. One night I was in a bar on the west side, called Paris Brest, a place which attracted immigrants and where you could speak French. I ordered a beer and took a big gulp. I thought I would lose my teeth, because the beer was so cold it froze my entire mouth. People who have gone to Europe tell me it is hard to adapt to warm beer. It goes the other way around, too.

One day on my way to work, I stopped for a hot dog at a street vendor near a fire station on 54th Street and 9th Avenue. The cart also sold pretzels, soda, and birch beer. I ordered a hot dog with sauerkraut and a birch beer. Oh boy, a hot dog and a nice cold beer, the good American way. When I started to drink the beer, I was convinced the guy was trying to poison me. I spit out the beer. Aside from the disgusting taste, I found out there was no alcoholic content!

Cooking at La Caravelle

After leaving La Potinière, I worked at La Caravelle. Bernard Millien, a fellow Breton, told me about the opening. In those days restaurants served 150 to 200 dinners for two services every night. The rush was for the 6:00 and 8:00 dinner services, the early service for those who planned to go to the theater afterwards.

There were a handful of such restaurants – La Caravelle, La Cote Basque, Le Pavillon, La Grenouille, and Lutece. They were truly good restaurants with very high standards for food and professional wait staff (though not as impeccable as at Lucas Carton in Paris). We offered classic French menus, prepared with the same methods as in France. I felt right at home, since everyone in the kitchen spoke French. Everyone, that is, but the Mexican dishwasher.

La Caravelle was opened in 1960 by Fred Decre and Robert Meyzen, who were restaurateurs, and by Chef Fessaguet. All of them had previously worked at Le Pavillon, a French restaurant on 57th Street that opened just after the 1939-1940 World's Fair and before the onset of World War II.

La Caravelle was the crème de la crème of New York restaurants. It was the best not only because of the food, but also the extraordinary service and attention to detail. The tradition of French restaurants in New York started when Henri Soule and Pierre Franey came to the World's Fair in 1939 to work the French Pavilion. For Americans who had not traveled abroad this was their first exposure to *haute cuisine* (literally "high cuisine"). At the time haute cuisine was synonymous with French classic. Today, the term is used more broadly and can be applied to any style of cuisine, so long as the common characteristics of careful preparation, elaborate service, critical acclaim, and, most importantly, obsessive attention to detail (and high price) are present.

Henri Soule and Pierre Franey did not want to return to France after the World's Fair, partly because of the political unrest, but they must have been attracted to the opportunities living in the United States might provide. When the fair closed and Le Pavillon opened, Henri Soule and his staff there only had non-permanent work visas. He took his staff with him to Niagara Falls, whereupon they walked across the bridge to Canada, then back into the United States, claiming to be war refugees. They were now legal!

When they left Le Pavillon for La Caravelle, the threesome brought in Jean Pages, a French artist and student of the famous artist, Raoul Duffy, to paint a mural that portrayed the Luxembourg Gardens on the left bank of Paris, featuring fashionably dressed people intermingled with common folk. Pages went on to become the creative and artistic director for *Vogue* magazine. Similar murals had been painted by Pages at La Cote Basque and at another restaurant in which I later worked, La Rotisserie Normande in New Haven, Connecticut. In addition to its famous murals, La Caravelle had red leather banquettes, which enhanced the aura of elegance.

La Caravelle transported you to another world. The ceilings were low, the lighting subdued, a real sense of ambience. When you entered there was the hat check girl to your left at the entrance to a large hallway. On each sides there were four tables, an area we referred to as Luxembourg and reserved for those, such as the elderly, who found it difficult to walk very far. Turning left, there were two more sets of tables of four on each side with a round table in the middle for large parties. Beyond that was an exclusive booth in the corner seating eight. People there could see who came in to the restaurant and, more importantly, be seen. At the tables there was seating on red leather banquettes. All tables had cream-colored tablecloths, nice china and silverware and glasses that, while not crystal, were of high quality. There were fresh flowers on each table. At the very end was the bar.

The kitchen at La Caravelle was the hottest kitchen I have ever worked, due to the fact that it was in the basement of a seven-floor building with the exhaust on the top floor and not much air intake. To its credit, it was well designed.

The night crew consisted of Maurice Pequet, in charge of the broiler and fish. I was in the middle of the kitchen, saucier and sauté cook. At the end of the line was an elderly Frenchman, Mr. Lafarque, who was the vegetable cook. Mr. Lafarque loved his Heineken beer, and after a few would tell us stories of all the beautiful women he had supposedly dated. With each beer they got more and more beautiful.

Yves Le Goff was butcher and garde manger, also from Brittany. The pastry chef, Jo Jo Keller, was from Alsace. Manny from Mexico was in charge of the pantry. The entire brigade was French. All of the wait staff were French, and all the bus boys were from Brittany. They were hard workers but had little food knowledge. I was told later that some of them resented me, because I did not have to start by washing dishes. Such attitudes are not uncommon in kitchens, but I had made sacrifices and worked hard to get formal culinary training and education.

The dinner menu was French classic, the same as we had in Paris, only at Lucas Carton there were fifteen in the kitchen for sixty customers, and we had to work lunch and dinner. At La Caravelle there were six of us in the kitchen for 250 customers for dinner only. We had to work harder in America.

For lunch and dinner we always had the special á la voiture, which means from the silver cart, or the special of the day. An advantage of this is that it would relieve the pressure off for a customer in a hurry by being served off the silver cart immediately. It also helped to have a good maitre d' who could regulate the flow of tickets going into the kitchen. Some of the specials I remember are saddle of lamb with *pomme sarladaise*, which are potatoes sliced and sautéed with truffles. There was also a stuffed veal breast served with mustard sauce on noodles, and a *quenelles de brochet* with *sauce nantua*, which is made with crayfish, very much like a lobster sauce. We also served roasted veal with champagne sauce accompanied by spinach. All specials were carved in front of the customer, usually by the owner, Robert Meyzen, but alternatively by the maitre d'.

On our á la carte menu we had *potage billibi*, a creamy mussel soup with saffron that can be served hot or cold. The mussels could also be served the following day with a light mustard sauce. There was *turbot grille, sole veronique* with white wine sauce and peeled grapes, *tournedos Rossini* with foie gras and truffle sauce. The á la carte menu was where you could really make money for the restaurant. One of the Kennedy's favorite dishes was pheasant souvaroff, with cognac, foie gras and truffles. The dish was served at the customer's table, and the aroma alone was worth the price of the meal.

When the owners left Le Pavillon, they brought with them an illustrious clientele, including Joseph Kennedy, Sr. I was working at La Caravelle when the Kennedys were customers. We were also patronized by the Vanderbilts, the Rockefellers and the Cabots. One day Joseph Kennedy, the ambassador to England, had a temper tantrum while I was in the kitchen. True to form, he always wanted the same table, a corner booth with seating for eight people called La Royale. Usually he came accompanied by several young ladies.

In the kitchen we referred to this booth as The Ace. In French, in card games the Ace is *As*, and it is also the same word for ass, so in the kitchen we referred to this table as The Ass, poking fun at the self-importance of many of who sat there.

On this particular day Joe Kennedy ordered a chocolate cake for someone's birthday, and in the confusion – perhaps the order was not taken properly – a white cake with chocolate frosting was made. When it came to the table, Kennedy flew into a rage, saying he had ordered a chocolate cake, adding that we were all a bunch of idiots.

Robert Meyzen, as one of the owners, walked over to Kennedy's table and said, "Your Excellency, I hope our friendship is not going to be broken because of a cake, but this check is on me. You can now leave, please go and pick up your coat."

Meyzen came in to the kitchen, telling Chef Fessaguet, "This is it, I just kicked Kennedy out." A few of us applauded.

Chef Fessaguet said, "Are you crazy? This is going to make all the headlines tomorrow."

Robert Meyzen said, "I don't care. Nobody can disrespect my establishment."

The following day Kennedy was back, which shows that the customer is not always right, but, even when he is wrong, you have to conduct yourself in a professional manner while standing your ground. It is a lesson I have never forgotten.

I worked the night shift at La Caravelle with Gerard Drouet, from Normandy. Robert Greault, who was a walking culinary encyclopedia, also worked there. If you needed to know which seven herbs were combined for a green turtle soup, he would rattle them off. Greault was a fabulous chef, but also a kind man who was interested in helping and mentoring others. He truly wanted to help us succeed.

There were seven in the kitchen brigade for lunch and seven for dinner. Many of those who worked alongside me later went on to do well in the culinary world, and I have often thought we should create an alumni association for those who worked there. Fernand Michaud went back to France an opened his restaurant in Grenoble, and Maurice Pequet became very successful in California, opening several restaurants in Los Angeles and then retiring to Provence. Gerard Drouet opened a very fancy restaurant called La Petite Marmite, near the United Nations, where he was the chef and the owner. Robert Greault, opened La Colline in Washington, D.C.

All French chefs who came to America were checked before

leaving the boat for references. But we all knew, even before we left France, to which restaurants we were heading. The Vatel Club, a French culinary club associated with Association de Culinaire de Paris, sent the best candidates to Fessaguet. The Vatel Club, which sadly no longer exists, was a vital networking center, especially for those of us new to the country.

At La Caravelle I was making $250 a week. For 1964 this was a very good salary, especially since our rent was only one week's worth of pay. At the same time, Anne-Marie was looking for a job, because she could not practice her profession as a nurse without a license. She found an ad in *France Amerique*, a French newspaper printed in New York, for a school that taught English. She only worked for one week, because it became clear it was a bogus school with incompetent instructors, that preyed on newly arrived immigrants to New York.

She took two jobs. In the morning she cleaned for a Belgian man with an apartment on Central Park. The place was filthy, so she was scrubbing floors on her hands and knees, cleaning his stove, and doing the laundry and ironing. Her work had to be completed before noon, and she was not allowed to eat there. Then, in the afternoon she worked for an elderly invalid lady twice her size to bathe her, give her all her shots, and do her cooking. Again, she was not allowed to eat there. All this for $1.25 an hour. She lost thirty pounds that summer. You are talking to the wrong person if you say that you can't find a job in this country. Later, she worked as a *dame de compagnie* – or lady's companion – to Lady Compton, a friend of Jackie Kennedy's. Neither of us were afraid to work hard. Slowly but surely, Anne-Marie and I felt as if we were getting ahead.

We had Sundays off, and we loved gospel music, so we found a church in Harlem where we went every week. One day it struck us that we were the only white folks in the assembly, but the people were very nice to us, especially when they realized we did not speak English. We also found some good jazz clubs in Harlem. I had grown up a teenager and young man listening to Sidney Bechet and other black jazz musicians who had gone to France to live, because there was not the racial prejudice and segregation as in America. But, once in New

York, I mostly listened to Elvis or the Supremes on the radio. There was not much time for music. I wanted desperately to go to Carnegie Hall, but I never had the time or money.

One day at work, everyone was talking about how they spent their weekend, and I mentioned we spent ours in Harlem. The others looked at me as if I was crazy. Later, they told me I was lucky to be alive, and whites were not welcome in Harlem. I did not understand what they were talking about and invited them to join us. Nobody took me up on the invitation.

Anne-Marie and I gained ground and saved money. It was wonderful to have our son, now fifteen months old, with us in America. Our progress learning English, however, was scant. Learning the language was one of our main goals, not just for convenience here, but for when we returned to France in two years. (This was forty-two years ago, and we are still here!) I made it a point not to patronize French bars on the West Side, run by fellow Bretons, because it was be too easy to carry on in my native tongue.

Once we established learning English needed to be a top priority, I began to look for restaurants where the staffs were not predominantly French. Since so many of the best restaurants in New York were French, this opened the prospect of looking outside of the city. This, in turn, led us to the next fork in the road.

Seafood with Cannellini Beans and Garlic Butter
Serves 4 – Prep time: 20 minutes – Cooking time: 15 minutes

The Story
Beans are underrated and you should always have a couple of cans in your pantry to add to a sauce in case you have put in too much water. In France, I made this dish with *flageolet* beans; they are smaller with a light green color. Unfortunately only high-end specialty food stores carry them. However, some farmers in Vermont are starting to grow them; it is a tradition in France to serve flageolet with roasted leg of lamb.

The Recipe
2 15-oz cans cannellini beans
12 16/20 shrimp, peeled and deveined
12 U-10 diver scallops (under 10 per pound)
1 lb cod filet, cut in bite size

Heat and drain the beans and reserve the stock. Place the stock into a pan, bring to a simmer, add the seafood and garlic butter. Cook for 3 minutes, add the beans. Check for doneness of the seafood.

Taste. Season. Taste.

Garlic Butter
3 shallots sliced
6 cloves of garlic chopped
8 ounces soft butter
½ bunch of Italian parsley chopped
1 tsp Pernod
1 Tbsp fresh ground black pepper
1 tsp salt

In a food processor place shallots, garlic, parsley and pulse several times, then add butter, salt, pepper, and Pernod. Mix well.

Moving Out of the Big Apple

Jean-Francois Vatel (1613-1671) served as chef de cuisine for Louis XIV. He made the ultimate sacrifice to his trade when he killed himself when an order of fish did not arrive on time. He threw his sword on the wall, and then ran himself into it. Talk about perfectionism and intensity!

The Vatel Club is a professional association of French-speaking chefs. When we decided to leave New York City, the Club found me a job in Hamden, Connecticut at The Carriage Drive. We did not have a car, nor licenses, yet this did not stop us from moving to New Haven. Once again, we were starting at the bottom. My English was rudimentary, though I could make myself somewhat understood through gestures. I only partly understood. I was afraid to take the orders, and I could not communicate with the employees. When people called on the phone, such as a purveyor to take an order, I could not say exactly what I wanted. It was a nightmare; each night I went home with a major headache. I felt stupid, without any self-esteem.

The Carriage Drive was opened by three brothers who owned a real estate company. They were very successful, but it was cash flow that attracted them to the restaurant business. There is always access to cash in restaurants, and there are different ways the money can be manipulated. Just like that, these three guys hired me, a French chef who could cook but not speak English. They also hired a manager who was crooked as a stick and a bartender who was in cahoots with the waitresses. The waitresses had been recruited in Aspen while the owners were there skiing. They were beautiful, but their looks were far superior to their table service. Welcome to America, the land of opportunity? It was a living hell working in such a restaurant where things were so crazy, the wait staff without a clue and me struggling to overcome the language barrier.

The restaurant was in an old carriage house, with a banquet room on the side. At first it was open only for lunch, with a simple menu consisting mostly of American sandwiches. Despite my training, I did not know how to make sandwiches. I was alone in the kitchen, except for the dishwasher Raymond, a French Canadian who was down on his luck. I surprised him by promoting him to pantry chef so that he could show me how sandwiches were made. His French was about as good as my English, but he could explain some of what I was saying to the staff purveyors, so he also became my interpreter.

The kitchen was huge, and I liked the fact you could see deliveries as they arrived. Many purveyors were shysters using a whole bag of tricks to skim money off the top by shorting orders. I knew their tricks and insisted on counting the items and weighing them. As you can imagine, this did not make me too popular.

For the night crew I hired students from the nearby Culinary Institute of America. Most of them had classroom instruction, but no hands-on training. I demonstrated how to do everything, which was helpful to them, but also covered up my poor language skills. As a group they were nice kids, and when I tried to say in something in English, they were very good about correcting me. While I was teaching them how to do everything in the kitchen, I was learning about cuts of meat from their classroom textbooks.

I hired a Mrs. Johnson as my dishwasher, and the first night she showed up with her little boys, Seth and Leon. She told me she had no babysitter. I said, "You have no babysitter, and I have no dishwasher," indicating that she could bring them to work if they behaved, and they did.

After a couple of weeks of operation, we started serving dinner, and then Sunday brunch. One Saturday night the dishwasher went home without finishing. I arrived the next morning to find a sink full of dirty pots in a half inch of grease. I knew I had hit bottom and, breaking my own rule about no crying in the kitchen, I broke down and sobbed. My head hurt from managing everything myself; I felt stupid, because I could not make myself understood. All the while I kept second-guessing our decision to come to America, comparing everything to the professional environment I had left behind in Paris.

I endured six months of this living hell, but at least made some connections with some French chef-instructors at the Culinary Institute of America, connections that proved very helpful down the road when I started my next job as the chef at La Rotisserie Normande on Chapel Street in New Haven. This was now 1967.

This lovely little restaurant was next to the Yale campus and was the best restaurant in town. The maitre d', Edmond, was a classy French guy who could sell anything that I put on the menu as a special dish. The waiters were very professional, and one of them, Walter, could remember the birthdays of all his customers. Edmond, in addition to his salesmanship, was so greedy that regular customers used to give him phony $5 and $10 bills to get a table or a better table. Edmond would discretely pocket the bogus bills and would have a fit later in the evening when he discovered the deception.

We may have been the best restaurant in town, but I needed some qualified help. I called one of my French connections at the Culinary Institute of America, and they sent me several students interns with decent training. One was Tony Seta, with whom I am still in touch. He is now Vice President for Research and Development for the Perkins Restaurant chain. We see each other two to three times a year, usually in New York, Chicago, or Boston at the food shows. We always have dinner together in the best restaurant in town. We make the obligatory trip down memory lane, but always end up talking about the same things – the basic cooking methods, work ethic, discipline and sacrifice, and how today's generation wants instant rewards. We're from a generation where you had to pay your dues!

Anne-Marie and I bought a house in Guilford, Connecticut, in 1965 with a $500 down payment. I had no credit, but I was making a good living. The price of the house was $15,000. Just before that, we set out to buy a Mercury Comet 202 and intending to pay for it with cash. I showed up at the dealership with $2,200, and the salesman said "What's this?" and I said

"That's $2,200 to buy my car." He said "No, no, I don't want your money, you can use your credit." I think most dealers today would be happy to accept cash.

New Haven in 1968 was in the midst of a civil rights movement spearheaded by the Black Panthers. There were numerous protests on campus. One day, I was sitting in my office at La Rotisserie Normande, and the phone rang. It was one of our regular customers on the line. "Hey Michel, we are going to celebrate at noon and need a six top."

I said, "Fine, sounds like a special occasion. Do you want me to make a special cake or dessert?"

He replied, "Haven't you heard? They killed that fucking nigger, Martin Luther King." It took my breath away to receive such terrible news in the same breath as the expression of such hatred.

Several weeks later I was driving to work on Interstate 95 when I heard of Bobby Kennedy's assassination on the radio. The whole world changed after John Kennedy, Martin Luther King, and Robert Kennedy were assassinated. I began to question whether I should stay in a country where such prejudice and violence were rampant. We missed our families, and our parents wanted to see their only grandson. We were torn between two countries. The choice was between one country where you worked hard but were able to purchase a house after fourteen months, and another where you can live in an apartment without running water and look for a new job every six months. We finally decided to return to France and put our house up for sale in January 1968.

I had now worked at La Rotisserie Normande for two years and was continuing my on-the-job learning of English. Anne-Marie was a waitress at a restaurant called La Crepe. Our son, Stephane, went to a babysitter when we both worked in the mornings. Anne-Marie repaid the people who babysat for Stephane by taking care of their children at night. Stephane was never left alone.

The bed was always warm. One of us would get in just as the other was getting out. One slept while the other worked, and then we switched. But we managed, and we even managed to save several thousand dollars. Work, work, work. Sleep. Work. Save every penny. Anne-Marie was learning English by watching "I Love Lucy" on TV. I was learning by shouting in the kitchen and always carrying a small dictionary.

We sold the house in Guilford, complete with furnishings, in January, planning to return to France at the end of August. We made our ship reservations, happy to be going home. We even planned to take our car, a 2 CV Citroen.

But in May of 1968 the new French Revolution began. All the working classes – from students to state employees to farmers and truck drivers – marched in the streets to demonstrate their unhappiness about the de Gaulle regime and working conditions. The country was paralyzed. The working people felt empowered and sensed the government's back was against the wall. Eventually, the government had to sit down and negotiate with unions, conceding better working conditions, social and economic reform, and more vacation time. I would have loved to have been there, because I emigrated due to the injustices of working twelve to fifteen hours a day, with no overtime or opportunity to get ahead.

In the midst of the chaos my mother-in-law communicated to us, saying, "I don't know your current plans, but maybe you should stay where you are."

We wanted to go home, all immigrants do. Unfortunately, now it seemed what we had left was no longer there. My mother-in-law was torn. She wanted us closer, but didn't know what we would be coming back to. Anne-Marie and I were at a crossroads, one which we have returned to many times over the years. Our destiny was at stake.

We decided it was not a good time to go back.

We had already sent our money to France. As of the last day of August, we had no place to live. One more time, we were without a home. Many people do not realize what it is like to be without a home, furniture, anything. It is very disconcerting and difficult to put into words. Sometimes the only reaction is to cry.

After a stint with some friends, we bought a new house in Guilford on Woodside Road. We had to buy all new furniture.

Tart Tatin

Serves 6

Prep time: 45 minutes

Cooking time: 20 minutes

The Story

This delicious pastry in which the taste of caramel is combined with the flavor of apples, cooked in butter under a golden crispy pastry crust, established the reputation of the Tatin sisters, who ran a restaurant in LaMotte, Beuron, at the beginning of the last century; it was served in Paris at Maxim's. When it was on the dessert cart, some customers ordered it before they ordered their entrées.

The Recipe

4 oz butter

6 oz sugar

12 Golden delicious apples, peeled, seeded,
    and quartered

2 Tbsp lemon juice

½ lb pie dough

In a 12" frying pan, melt the butter and add the sugar. Make a light caramel. Turn off the heat, arrange quartered apples vertically starting on the edge and fill the pan. Turn on the heat and add more apples until the pan is full, then cover it with a plate until the caramel reaches the edge of the pan. Turn off the heat. Roll out the pie dough and place it on top of the apples, seal the edge. Place in a 350° oven for 20 minutes. Let cool.

Note: this tart will be better if made the day before serving because the apples need to settle. Reheat slowly to loosen the caramel and turn the tart upside down. Serve with vanilla ice cream or whipped cream.

The Yale Years

I decided to put my restaurant career on hold and applied for a job at Yale University in 1968. As before, I heard about the job through my personal connections. I did not have a formal resumé, but got the job through word of mouth recommendations.

Three days after I started, the food service employees went on strike. Because of this, I had the opportunity to show the people that hired me that, not only could I cook, I knew how to order food and to teach to cook. This turned out to be a serendipitous break for me, because when the strike was over and normalcy returned, I started working on the overall food plan for the school. There were twelve residential colleges, each with their own kitchens, not your typical college dining halls. A citadel of great architecture, the dining halls of Yale resembled old English dining halls more than college dining halls. Each college even had its own individual china and sterling silver.

The food plan for the school was huge and presented many challenges. There was disorder and inconsistency, because each kitchen manager was writing his own menus and recipes. There was no standardization. My task was to develop a recipe file for the food service and write a menu cycle with the help of three dietitians. This was a big undertaking. In the process, they wanted me to make the food healthier and more interesting.

I never thought I would be part of the food and culture of America, but in terms of history, I was witnessing it firsthand. Just by being on the campus, I witnessed the students' protests against the war in Vietnam. The student protests at Kent State could just as easily have happened at Yale.

On May Day, 1970, the National Guard was in New Haven. This was, in part, the result of public statements by President Kingman Brewster that the Black Panthers could never get a fair trial in New Haven. Classes were cancelled in anticipation of protests and possibly riots. Brewster responded by opening the campus to everyone. The thousands of protesters were fed for three days on a menu of salad, granola, bread, and bug juice (Kool-Aid). And this also meant for three days I played poker and Frisbee while mingling with the crowd!

Brewster started to admit worthy but impoverished Latino and Asian students as well as African-Americans. This created a stir with the old guard (know as the Old Blues) at Yale, and was considered radical in the Ivy League schools.

My biggest project at Yale was to convert classical French dishes into institutional food, taking into consideration factors like available equipment and even more importantly, students' tastes. Over the next few years I tested recipes for 100 or even 200 portions of classical recipes. (If you multiply a recipe for 100 times two, it does not always work, especially when it comes to spices!)

My test kitchen was in the Hall of Graduate Studies. Once or twice a week a panel of students, cooks, managers, and the dietitian would taste a dish I had developed, recipes ranging from macaroni and cheese to coq au vin to minestrone soup to crêpes suzettes. The hardest part was to train the cooks, because they thought it would make more work for them. Eventually, I convinced them to try some different cooking methods and menus. (People resist change!)

The food became better and better, and we continued to work on cost control. We started a large salad bar and served more fruit. Carmen Cozza, the head football coach, told me he used the reputation for Yale's excellent food to recruit football players. Two Yale players who went on to become professionals, undoubtedly fueled by my food, were John Spagnole, a tight end for the Philadelphia Eagles, and Gary Fencik, a safety for the Chicago Bears. My boss, Al Dobie, the Director of Food Service at Yale, received the Silver Plate award by the National College of University Food Service for "best food in a university."

As a growing segment of the student body became more health conscious, there were still many who wanted a Shepard's Pie and beef stew. I started to develop vegetarian dishes, serving soybean patties cooked in V-8 juice, and creating recipes using kasha and tofu while eliminating animal fat. We cooked fish with an Asian touch, and also served a lot of curry, which became popular due to the Beatles's embrace of Indian culture.

The Commons, the freshman dining hall, was now serving 250 to 300 students on the natural food line. When we had steak night maybe fifty of the health-conscious group would show up and go straight for the baked potatoes and sour cream.

After the oil embargo in 1973, beef, which had been the staple of the American diet, became very expensive. Al Dobie called me to his office and told me we had done a great job with the new recipe file, but I had to come out with items that were less expensive, such as casseroles, so we could make budget. We were budgeted to lose $1 million, no small potatoes even for Yale. So I started thinking about the problem and went back to what I ate when I was a kid. *Hey, cod cheeks!* I said to myself. My father used to get them by the barrel as a present from the fishermen back from Newfoundland. My father had wanted to put me on a fishing boat that would be gone for up to three months. *No, thanks*, I made it clear that I would rather sleep in a barn than go off fishing in Newfoundland.

So, I called a guy named Bart, who was one of our fish purveyors in Boston.

"Hey, Bart, how much for fish cheeks?"

"For you Michel, what it costs me in overtime, about 80 cents a pound."

"Deal!"

I ordered hundreds of pounds and made some delicious casseroles which the students loved. The *Yale Daily News* and the *New Haven Register* got wind of our money-saving creativity that was going to help us make budget.

I received a call from the *New Haven Register*, wanting to learn what we had done. I checked with Al Dobie to see if I could be interviewed about the subject, and he said, "No problem, go ahead." A woman reporter from the paper came with a photographer to interview me. She was intrigued by the fact that I came to Yale after working in such culinary capitals as New York, Paris, and Lausanne.

Michel Le Borgne during the Yale years

She asked me, "Chef, tell me what you have done to save money?"

My answer was, "Well, it is very simple. I remember what I was eating at home after World War II, which was cod cakes twice a week. Unfortunately, in this country, you make cat food with that."

The following day, there was a big headline, along with my picture, in the *New Haven Register* which read "Yale Feeds Cat Food to Their Students." The Associated Press picked up the story and within a short period of time, parents from all over the world were calling the dining hall service.

My lesson was to be very careful what you say to reporters. I never had said that we fed cat food to students. I called that reporter and invited her to lunch, but she declined. I wonder why! The funniest part of this was that when the students on campus saw me, they would *meow, meow*. I thought this was pretty funny.

Wine was becoming more popular in America. Food tastes better with wine and vice versa, which is what I call "the French paradox." The French eat more cheese, butter, and cream per capita than anyone in the world, but also have, after the Japanese, the lowest rate of heart attacks. This is thanks to red wine which lowers cholesterol.

There is less obesity in France than America. People walk a lot more and do not drive around the block three times to find a parking spot as close to the building as possible. The French eat smaller portions and make a meal last. Eating is more social and important than chowing down a big meal in record time. They eat to live, not live to eat.

Michel Guerard and Louis Outhier are French chefs credited with starting *cuisine minceur*, known here as *nouvelle cuisine*. It's a misleading term, because until we come up with a dish using a five-legged rabbit, we will not have invented anything new! Guerard and Outhier emphasized the freshness of the product and used more seasonal ingredients. They also promoted the use of fresh herbs, and thickening sauce with vegetables instead of heavy cream. To me their most important innovation was an emphasis on smaller portions.

In the United States at this same time, Alice Waters in California was demanding organic foods and inventing wildly creative salads. Some people thought she was eccentric, but she was passionate, funny, instructive, and rich with common sense. Further south in Los Angeles, Wolfgang Puck kicked it up one more notch when he opened Chinois on Main Street. It was the place to see and be seen for all of Hollywood, and that was perfect advertising for his food and menu.

Lydia Shire in Boston was changing the eating habits of the blue-blooded Brahmins. She was the first one to popularize serving rare tuna on salade niçoise. *Mon Dieu*, this was revolutionary! She also mastered Asian and classic styles of cooking, and had a soft spot for inneroffal (pig's feet), sweetbreads (thymus glands), kidneys, calf brains, tripe (stomach), and tongue. These were considered food for poor people – but for true gastronomes they are soul food! The spirit of change was everywhere in the culinary world.

Between 1970 and 1980 I developed and tasted 1100 recipes at Yale, an accomplishment of which I am very proud. I could not have done this without the help of dietitians Karen Dougherty, Anne Van Dyke, Jean Jones, and Pat Glynn. A student, Mimi Lines, was the proofreader for the recipe cards.

One of the residential college masters had the idea of serving breakfast in bed to all the freshmen who lived on the Old Campus. The dietitians and I looked at each other, thinking *This guy is a nut*. But we told him to give us a week to think about it.

After he left, we all agreed this was a serious challenge, which would take some serious planning. What motivated us most was curiosity about what the students' reactions would be! We agreed to do it on the condition that we would not be the ones knocking on the students' doors. A student named John agreed to coordinate the delivery door-to-door.

On the morning after exams were finished, in each entrance of every building on the Old Campus, we delivered breakfast trays of scrambled eggs, bagels, cream cheese and lox, orange juice and coffee, served with the *New York Times* and a cigar for the male students and a red carnation for the female students. The telephone company made a lot of money that day with the kids describing their breakfast in bed. Our feat was covered by the *New York Times*, but not the *New Haven Register*. What goes around comes around!

Twice a year we had incredible events built around food and music. One was "April in Paris," where we made crêpes suzettes for four thousand people. Another was called "Star Trek," and yet another "Soul Food Night." Students were involved, volunteering for decorating and helping with the music. They would show up for the event dressed to kill, in keeping with the theme. At "A Luau in Springtime" a student from Hawaii told her parents about the event, and they sent, air freight on a Boeing 707, a cargo of native food and dress. They sent everything except the pigs. The party was a blast.

At Yale we served several chiefs of state, Bill and Hillary Clinton when they were at the Law School, future presidents (George Bush) and governors (George Pataki and Howard Dean). I was able to take advantage of the university facilities such as the Payne Whitney gym. I was a fierce racquetball player, but not very good. Still, it kept me in physical shape and helped relieve some of the stress that comes with this business.

Graduations and class reunions were always high spots on the social calendar, but not so much as food was concerned, "Old Blues" (the alumni) still wanted surf & turf, cheesecake, and plenty of liquor.

I met Meryl Streep on a Saturday night when I was managing at Yale Cabaret to make some extra money. There was already a buzz that she was going to be a star. I had breakfast with Bill Bradley from the *Washington Post*. While I wanted to ask him about Watergate, he, being an investigative reporter, wanted to know how my path led me to Yale.

In the mid-1970s I was invited by *House Beautiful* to be part of a photo shoot with the theme "Christmas Sweets from Many Lands." The shooting held in July in the 7th floor, 42nd Street apartment of Ellen McAulley, one of the food editors. Ellen did not believe in air conditioning, and it was a hot day. I made a chocolate yule log, or *bûche de Noël*. I was very proud of my bûche, until the powder sugar, simulating snow, and butter cream started to melt under the photographer's lights. I told the photographer, "Hurry up," and he replied, "Don't worry, Chef, we will fix it." I answered back, "That is impossible." But he explained, "We will fix it by putting a rolling pin in the freezer, and then you will decorate the bûche the same way you decorated the sponge cake. No one, except me, will know that it is a rolling pin." Now you, too, know some of the tricks of the photographer's trade.

As time passed the food services at Yale became more consistent and systematized. More and more the place was on automatic pilot. A typical day began with reading the newspaper to see how much beef and other foods cost and doing some paper work, not my strong suit. After shooting the breeze with the girls in food services, perhaps I would go rattle someone's cage, followed by two hours of racquetball, then lunch with the students in the Hall of Graduate Studies. Many of the students became my friends. I would then check two or three kitchens, do a health inspection, and then head home before the traffic jam. I had learned much at Yale and thoroughly enjoyed my time there, but increasingly it was clear that the challenge was gone.

Sautéed Salmon with Catsup Sauce
Serves 4

Prep time: 15 min

Cooking time : 10 min

The Recipe
4 6-oz salmon skinless center cut

1 Tbsp vegetable oil

2 oz butter

1 lemon peeled, supremed, seeds removed, diced small

1 ripe tomato peeled, seeded, diced small

1 Golden Delicious apple peeled and diced

2 Tbsp capers

1/3 c catsup

Place a medium-size sauté pan on medium heat , brush with oil and place salmon in the pan, season. Cook for 2 minutes on one side, turn over and cook another 2 minutes, remove and place on hot plates.

While the salmon cooks, place butter in another sauté pan and cook until brown, or until it does not sizzle any longer. Add at once lemon, tomato, apple, capers, and heat well, then add the catsup, bring to a simmer, pour over the salmon .

Learning about Taste Buds

It was 1979, and I needed a new challenge. My racquetball game was not getting better. I could, however, outsprint all the kids in the neighborhood, including my son, Stephane, now a junior in high school. He had his driving license, and was increasingly independent, so I went looking for a new job.

In the summer I took a leave of absence from Yale and did consulting for Seabrook Farms in New Jersey. I worked with two scientists whose knowledge of food astounded me. They explained many things that helped me to become a better-rounded chef. They explained what happens to food when heat is applied. I learned how combinations of food interact, and how taste buds work, what creates the particular tastes of sweet and sour, bitter and salt. At eighteen I knew everything. Now, at forty I was just beginning to learn. Today, I am still learning and intend to never stop.

Here's an example of how a smattering of scientific knowledge can shed new light on a food phenomenon. Many people turn up their noses at catsup, but it was one smart guy who put together tomatoes, vinegar, salt, sugar, and water as sauce for his French fries. Vinegar cuts the fat feeling or greasiness, while sugar and salt heighten the flavor. I used this knowledge to develop an original recipe for salmon with catsup (see page 102).

I loved the consulting work, and was learning a great deal, but they wanted me to move to California. My son was going into his senior year in high school, and I thought it important that he finish high school with his friends. When my sabbatical was over, I returned to my work at Yale.

Maple Crème Brulée

Serves 6

Prep time: minutes

Cooking time: minutes

The Story

Lately this beautiful simple dessert has become the *souffre-douleur* of amateur pastry chefs, and on dessert menus appear: grapefruit crème brulée, artichoke crème brulée, green pepper corn, lavender, etc. At NECI Commons on Church Street in Burlington we served Maple Crème Brulée, #1) I think we can substitute maple syrup for sugar, #2) we are in Vermont, #3) customers love it.

The Recipe

½ C milk
8 egg yolks
2 C heavy cream
½ C maple syrup, amber grade B
1 vanilla bean, split lengthwise
¼ C sugar

Preheat the oven to 325°.

In a sauce pot heat the cream, milk and vanilla bean. Bring to a boil then let cool to room temperature. Remove but save the vanilla bean. Combine the maple syrup and the egg yolks then temper then with the heavy cream. Pour into baking dishes. Line a baking pan with a towel then place the baking dishes on top. Add water and bake for 35-40 minutes. Remove from the oven, cool and refrigerate.

Serving: Uniformly sprinkle sugar on top of each pan and caramelize with a blow torch.

Note: the towel on the bottom of the baking dish is to prevent the water from boiling.

The Interview, the Idea

Our family had been vacationing in the small Vermont town of West Barnet. Typically, we would go three times a year, including the 4th of July, fall foliage season, and on Christmas. We even bought a beautiful piece of land. We loved the scenic Northeast Kingdom. It was a great place to visit for three days, but after that we were ready to return home. I also enjoyed the down-to earth people. You won't impress a Vermonter with a BMW, but if you have ten cords of wood split for the winter, you might earn their respect.

In March of 1980, I was doing a cooking demo in Hartford, Connecticut. I mentioned to someone I had just met that I was looking for a job. He told me he had seen someone in *Restaurant News* looking for an executive chef to open a cooking school in Vermont. *Why Vermont?* I asked myself. There was nothing there. But when I went home and mentioned this to Anne-Marie, she said I should call at once.

But call where? And to whom?

In 1980 we had live telephone operators. (Imagine that!)

The operator asked, "What city, please?"

I told her to try Burlington, but had no name to give her. I only knew I was looking for a cooking or culinary school. There was nothing. I decided to pass on Rutland and suggested she try Montpelier.

"Yes, we have a New England Culinary Institute."

I called on a Saturday. I introduced myself and asked if they were still taking applications for the executive chef position. I was told they were not taking any more applications, but they would take mine. When I arrived at my office at Yale on Monday, I asked Karen and Pat, the dietitians, to write my resumé. It was the first time I had ever applied for a job … forty-one years old. All of my previous jobs had come by word of mouth.

When the New England Culinary Institute received my resume, I was asked to come to Montpelier for an interview on March 13. Thirteen is my lucky number, not only is March 13 my birthday, I graduated from school May 13 and arrived in the United States on May 13. This was a good omen.

I tried to dress appropriately by wearing a gabardine suit and cowboy boots. The office was on the third floor above the Thrush Tavern, a favorite hang-out for journalists and political junkies. (It's just down the street from the golden dome of the Vermont State House.) The Culinary Institute had five tiny rooms, all with slanted ceilings, so I had to duck frequently to not hit my head. And I am not a tall guy! There was an all-pervading smell of the hamburger grease wafting up from the Thrush Tavern.

I arrived with no expectations. I had never had a formal interview. Pat and Karen coached me, advising me to be myself, but they said if there was a higher chair in the room, to go for it, so I would have more control. A higher chair means more power.

The dimly lit office with its low ceilings did not make a great impression. The first person I saw was Florence, the administrative assistant. She politely asked me to have a seat, as I was early. I am always early. I sat down at the very end of an uncomfortable, secondhand couch. She went into another room and announced my arrival. I noticed there were not even any magazines on the coffee table.

I was introduced to a tall woman, Bonnie, who was the personnel director. After talking to Bonnie for a minute, Florence then brought me to a somber room where I met Fran Voigt, the President. He was wearing a bow tie, which struck me as out of place in Vermont. Next I met Vice-President and the Academic Program Director, Howard, who sported a Che Guevara mustache and spoke with a southern accent. Last of all, I met Ron Marinelli, Director of Food Services for Vermont National Life (an insurance company) and the culinary advisor for New England Culinary Institute. In front of them were a card table and a barstool.

I made a beeline for the bar stool, so then I was looking

down on the other four. After exchanging pleasantries they asked me why I would consider leaving such a prestigious job at Yale.

"Time to move on, I need a new challenge," I said. Fran had a clipboard and was writing down everything I said. Then came the million-dollar question.

If you were going to open a cooking school, how would you train the students?

"The answer is very simple," I replied. "I would train them just the way I learned: Hands on."

Evidently, these were the magic words they were looking for. I could see it in their eyes.

Then it was my turn to ask questions. *What had they been doing before they started to think about opening a cooking school?*

Fran had been a director of programs at Goddard College. (It was not at all clear to me what a director of programs did.) Howard worked at a community school in Richmond, Virginia, then at the Community College when he moved to Vermont.

Why would three guys with no food background want to open a cooking school?

Fran tried to brew beer, but his neighbors (and taste testers) politely advised him he should try something else. He considered raising fall deer (miniature deer whose meat is considered a delicacy), but before that venture got off the ground he read in the *Wall Street Journal* that in the year 2000, there would be a shortage of qualified cooks.

That's it! I'll open a cooking school Fran said to himself.

"Do you know about cooking?" I asked.

"No."

"Do you know how to run a restaurant?"

"No."

"Basically, you don't have much background in the food business, is that correct?"

"Correct," said Fran, adding, "but we have done our homework." By this he meant they had visited several cooking schools, posing as reporters. They had also talked to renowned chefs to ask their opinions on the other culinary schools. They discovered that the culinary students at the other schools thought of themselves as chefs, but often lacked basic skills such as how to use a knife.

Fran's father, a surgeon, told him that he learned his profession not in the classroom, but in the operating room. You learn by doing. This is as true for cooking as brain surgery. So here we were, four guys from vastly different backgrounds, with one idea in common – teaching cooking through hands-on learning.

Chef Michel, 1980

Making my Goodbye Rounds at Yale

Graduation is special for students and parents. It was also important for me. It meant saying good-bye to students on financial aid who worked in the dining halls and had become friends. Some were dishwashers and some moved up to be assistant managers. Most were very bright kids, and I am fortunate to still be touch with several of them – W.C. Gray, Mimi Lines, Alain Noirey, and Paco, a handsome Indian-Mexican.

In May of 1980 I especially did not want to miss graduation, because it would be my last at Yale, as I had accepted a position with the New England Culinary Institute in Vermont. B.B. King received an honorary degree. After the ceremonies, I made my farewell rounds. There were a lot of tears. There was a lot of mugging for the camera. That afternoon was overflowing with memories and mixed emotions. I was sad to leave Yale, but excited about my new venture, opening a cooking school, from the ground floor up.

Roasted Cod and Shallots with Lentils
Serves 4

The Story

No big story about this one except that the cod was the fish for the poor people, now it is the fish of choice. And I like lentils.

The Recipe

1 lb Lentils

4 6-ounce boneless, skinless cod fillets

1 onion diced

$1/3$ cup olive oil

1 carrot diced

bouquet garni

12 oz shallots, unpeeled and trimmed at both ends

salt

Soak lentils overnight and cover with cold water to 2 inches above the lentils.

Add onion, carrots, and bouquet garni. Simmer for 20 minutes or until tender. Add salt to taste, remove bouquet garni. Reserve 1 cup of cooking liquid and drain.

Preheat oven to 300°F.

Put shallots in ovenproof skillet and add 1 Tbsp of olive oil. Roast in oven 15 to 20 minutes. Let cool, peel shallots and reserve.

Place cod in ovenproof skillet, brush with olive oil, and sprinkle with salt. Roast for 10 to 12 minutes. While cod is roasting, place one cup of cooked lentils in a blender.

Turn blender on and slowly add reserved cooking liquid and $1/3$ cup olive oil. Add purée back to cooked lentils.

To serve:

For each serving pour 1 cup of lentils into a warmed plate.

Place cod fillet in center and garnish with roasted shallots.

The Opening of New England Culinary Institute

Before signing my contract with the New England Culinary Institute, I was given a free booth and invited to participate at the Boston Food Show. The booth was next to the dumpster with a seagull on the side! My purpose was to promote the school. It was cold and drafty in the exposition hall. See what you get for nothing? We had very little literature or display material, primarily a picture of a local lawyer named Steamer, dressed up in a floppy chef's hat, holding a tray of food. We were trying to recruit students, but did not yet even have a kitchen. The plan was to make an arrangement with the Tavern Motor Inn to take over their kitchen facility.

I honestly do not know what compelled me to join this venture. I was either irresponsible or crazy.

John and Fran, who were with me at the Food Show, invited me to a Chinese restaurant, Joyce Chen's, for dinner. This was one of the best restaurants in Boston in 1980. Anyone who has ever opened a restaurant or a hotel will tell you *never again!* Even with the greatest plan and staff, something will inevitably go wrong. Here I was, opening not a restaurant but an entire cooking school in an unfamiliar town, with students soon coming from as far as Alaska. I had two weeks to contact the purveyors (with whom we had no credit) and write the menu. I was dealing with salesmen who had no idea what they were selling, but who just wanted your business. They'd promise a certain grade of meat, then send a lesser grade. I had to do purchasing, receiving, and storage, not to mention teaching and menu creation. Thinking back, I do not know how I survived. Perhaps it was a combination of stubbornness and pride.

I wrote the menu according to the curriculum we were teaching. Our goal was to be accredited in two years. Writing the menu for the students was not difficult. I had to make

111

sure everyone had good knife skills, and learned all the cooking methods and basic sauces. I did not anticipate, however, the need to educate the palates of our local customers. Our competition was The Horn of the Moon, a small but good vegetarian restaurant, and the Lobster Pot, where you could have all you could eat for $5. Their salad bar featured such items as beans "fresh from the can." Further up the road was The Stockyard, a restaurant by the Winooski River, housed in an old railroad car. It was known for its red meat.

I had to figure out what the Montpelier population would accept, and initially that was meat and potatoes. Thus, I put pot roast on the menu while teaching braising to the students. Vegetables had to be cut uniformly to cook uniformly. I put tournee potatoes (potatoes with seven sides, like a football), because it provided the opportunity to teach knife skills.

I had an assistant instructor who soon left. I was alone for the next three weeks, preparing lunch and dinner with three students in each two-week learning "block." This was "learning by doing" in the extreme!

I have been involved with restaurant openings, but this one was unique. Nothing was familiar – the environment, the kitchen, the equipment. Add to the mix students who in some cases had never even cooked an egg. Our wait staff was inherited from the Tavern Motor Inn, and were none too enthusiastic about having the school take over.

...

It was a nightmare.

The only silver lining is that we were not too busy. One time a student, Tony, was on the grill. His job was to make pancakes and fry eggs at the same time. Very quickly he got into trouble, and I needed to take over. I had not cooked breakfast for many years, but, like bicycling, it is a skill you do not forget. I realized then that doing is easier than teaching. I had to learn to teach.

A good example of this is instructing someone how to do the mise en place – preparing your ingredients in advance – an essential skill. Doing this is hard enough, but teaching it ... *mais oui* ... much harder. Don't ask me what was on the lunch menu back then, but I am sure that it was very, very, simple; I was already in over my head.

Mid-service I had an incident with a pot washer named Mike. He was a World War II veteran who walked around with a pint of brandy in his back pocket. I asked him quite nicely to wash a few dishes.

He said, "Oh no, I am a pot washer, not a dishwasher."

I said, "We are not that busy, so can you wash a few dishes?"

"No, no, I only wash pots," he replied.

"Okay, if you don't want to do it, you might as well punch out and go home now," which he did. Then it hit me … now, I had no pot washer and no dishwasher. Lesson: do not fire anyone until you have hired a replacement.

I do no know if I was motivated by panic or inspiration, but I called Fran, the President, and said "Fran, if you want New England Culinary Institute to last very long, you'd better come down here in your brand new sneakers, because I am going to teach you how to wash pots and pans and wash dishes at the same time." Five minutes later Fran appeared (in his white sneakers). I gave him an apron and showed him the drill. You wash, you rinse, and you sanitize. That's it for pots and pans. Next I showed him how to wash dishes. Put them in that giant machine, push the green button, and the dishes come out nice and dry. You just stack them and put them back where they belong. This was Fran's introduction to food service, and he handled it well. I think Fran retired those famous sneakers, thinking it might be bad luck if he wore them again.

The dinner menu back then was very short. It started with minestrone soup so the students could practice knife skills and learn how to cook dry beans properly. Next came a seasonal salad so they learned how to clean greens properly and to make a simple emulsified dressing. Shrimp cocktail was offered so they would learn to cook shrimp properly. (How many times have you been served rubbery shrimp?) Melon and prosciutto was also on the menu, because it is hard to screw up.

The fish entrée was sautéed filet of flounder almondine. It was popular and allowed me to teach sautéing. For poultry we served roasted chicken with tourneed potatoes and green beans persillade and for beef, broiled sirloin steak with bernaise sauce. For dessert there was tart tartin, an upside down apple pie.

Despite its simplicity, this menu utilizes all the basic cooking methods which a chef should master. It is not what you do, but how you do it.

When people ask what my favorite dishes are, I always say I just want *a roasted chicken cooked properly, a nice salad, some roquefort and a bottle of wine*. That was my teaching philosophy, so my students learned how to roast the chicken properly.

I had not made tournée potatoes for twelve years so my first six were not perfect. At the end of the day, I told Fran that I just couldn't handle three meals by myself. I suggested he call Kay Voorhees, who until recently had been the breakfast cook, to ask her to come back.

Kay doesn't get the credit she deserves, but in my opinion, New England Culinary Institute would not be what it is today without her. That lady was a professional short order cook, amazing to watch. Her feet would never move. She was also great at whipping out club sandwiches and BLTs, things that I was not good at. She was also a good and patient teacher. Once a week we had the Rotary Club for lunch, usually soup, sandwich, and a salad. Kay showed one student how to clean a head of iceberg lettuce, by lightly pounding the lettuce on the table, twisting and removing the core, then turning the lettuce upside down to drain the water. A couple of weeks later she had coleslaw on the menu and asked the same student to prepare the green and red cabbage. The student took the head of cabbage and pounded it on the table and promptly dislocated his shoulder.

It's no surprise that Kay became a fixture at NECI for many years.

...

One day we lost a student because it was too hot. If you can't stand the heat of the kitchen, get out. I thought back to what Chef Bernard had drilled into my head, how to be mentally strong and accustomed to physical discomfort. Having grown up during World War II, dealing with shortages and the hard-ships of men who left their families, I have learned to deal with things as they are, and not the way you would like them to be.

I remember at the Hotel Printania in Dinard in Brittany when I was about sixteen. It was my second stage – *mon deuxième étage* – my turn to do the omelet service. We removed the rings from the stove to get the flame hotter to make the omelets. After an hour there, I had to change jackets, as mine was soaking wet. It was probably about 125 degrees in that kitchen, but it did not slow me down. In fact, I never thought about the heat, because I was on such an adrenaline rush. When things are not easy, rise to the occasion. Some may think this is perverse, but this is why I love cooking and being in this challenging business. If you can't take the heat, goes the cliche, get out of the kitchen. But for me, the hotter it gets, the more I sweat, the more I thrive.

I hired Michael Prevost, a cook I knew from my days at Yale. He both saved my life and added a new dimension to the cur-riculum by teaching buffet and banquet, neither of which are strong suits for me.

The core group of students consisted of Bill Shippen, Peter Roy, Marc Scovolle, Clark Green, Rita Sanford and Tony Klimitz. Peter Roy was actually recruited by his father, a farmer in north-ern Vermont who was watching a TV show about a restaurant and yelled out to Peter, "They get $25 for lunch. You can make more money by doing that than by staying here. That's it, son! You are going to be a chef."

The wait staff predicted we would fail during foliage season, when tourists flock to Vermont. *You will never make it with the students,* they said. But this only made me more determined.

We served breakfast, lunch, and dinner to two or three bus loads of tourists a day, plus the walk-in customers. I fine-tuned the menu accordingly. Breakfast was a buffet, which seemed like it would be easy, except the students typically burned six to eight pans of bacon every morning before I could serve one slice! I bought a timer, and hung it around the neck of the student in charge of the bacon. This actually solved the burnt bacon problem.

We survived the foliage season and went out to celebrate at a nightclub called The Red Fox. We promptly renamed it *The Dead Fox*, because it was so funky, not funky as in "cool." Business at the restaurant slowed down after Columbus Day, and the first term ended after Thanksgiving. I drove back to Connecticut after dinner to see my wife and son, my first weekend off in six months.

...

During the summer and fall of 1980 Anne-Marie and Stephane came and visited me every other weekend. We always stayed in West Barnet in Vermont's remote Northeast Kingdom with our friends Minou and Kerwyn Daniels, who had moved from Connecticut several years earlier. This provided a welcome break from my hotel room at the Tavern Motor Inn in Montpelier. I doubled as the dorm proctor.

We looked for a rental so that we could all be together, but there were several obstacles. Our house in Connecticut was on the market, but with mortgage rates at 18% prospective buyers were few and far between. Finally we found a house for rent in West Barnet right on Harvey's Lake. It was a seasonal rental, fairly reasonable, that would become available on November 1 when the owner left to spend the winter in Arizona. (This should been a clue.) I would still commute to Montpelier, but it was better than a lonely hotel room.

It was a hard winter even by Vermont standards. Our "bargain" rental disappeared when we saw our first oil bill. The house was barely insulated, and the furnace ran 24 hours a day to keep the house at 60 degrees. I wrapped myself in an electric blanket to watch TV, and we did have a lovely view of the frozen lake, but on Christmas Day it was minus 35! Welcome to Vermont!

...

Stephane departed to ski the Alps for two months, and Anne-Marie moved up permanently. She found a job in St. Johnsbury, which helped with the oil bills, but we were still questioning our decision to move to Vermont. We loved it during summer and fall, but winter was barely survivable.

I managed to drive into a ditch not once, but three times. During the state's dreaded Mud Season I could not take the short cut by Max Mountain, lengthening my commute to Montpelier by an additional fifteen minutes. It didn't take long for me to get burned out on this routine. Finally, Anne-Marie found a job at Central Vermont Hospital in Berlin, a town adjacent to Montpelier, which gave us an excuse to move closer to NECI.

Decent apartments were scarce, so we broke down and bought a beautiful old house on Liberty Street. Now, I could walk to work, and Anne-Marie only had a ten-minute drive to the hospital.

Despite the financial suicide of having two mortgages, life was getting better. Spring turned into summer, and Stephane returned from the Alps with a suitcase full of ski trophies. He did not want to go to college yet, but helped me when I needed an extra pair of hands in the kitchen. I quickly took note of his great knife skills and his natural kitchen awareness. (I had never showed him anything.) Over the past few years we had cooked together and it was fun. I finally asked him the million dollar question: *Would he consider cooking for a career in the kitchen?*

His answer was immediate and definitive. *NO.* I was devastated. I had allowed myself to fantasize about what we could accomplish. His refusal made for one of the worst days in my life, but I could not argue with his reasoning. He did not want to be in a profession where he might be forever known as "Chef Michel's son."

He joined the Air Force that September. Today, he is very successful, living in Dover, New Hampshire with his wife Sue and sons Kyle and Alec. No one refers to him as "Chef Michel's son."

...

The school survived its first year of operation. Recruiting was good, and we enrolled a student from California, Leah Cohen, who was a great gymnast, as well as Michael Papandrea, a former running back in high school. Another student, Danny

Michaud, came from Maine and now teaches at New England Culinary Institute. Tim Corcoran came from Philadelphia and later accompanied me to the Maryland Crab Cooking Contest.

Four students returned for the second residency. We had to let go an instructor who graduated first in his class from a big culinary school, because he could not make a potato leek soup. (There were a few other reasons, too.) He then sued the school for wrongful termination! He showed up in court with The *Larousse Gastronomique,* a reference book for the culinary industry, to prove that, indeed, he could make potato leek soup. The judge thought this was pretty funny and dismissed the case. I felt a little sorry for him, because he was depressed and could not find a job.

His dismissal meant we had to adjust the curriculum, needing someone to teach culinary history, wine and cheese. This was too much for me, so I asked Anne-Marie to come to the rescue. She took on the challenge for the whopping compensation of $300, payable at the end of the semester. This was an enormous monetary sacrifice, but one from which we never looked back. We both threw ourselves into the fledgling program and within two years the school had become our life, the students our foster children. The living room of our Montpelier home became the study hall, our refrigerator the local bar and grocery store.

Not all was food, wine, and laughter. During the busiest time of foliage season I had an ugly little incident with a student in the kitchen. In the heat of service I demanded of Sam from Alaska to work a little faster. He told me to go fuck myself. A chef does not accept this, especially from an eighteen year old. Without thinking, I hit him with a head butt, cutting him (and myself, too) above the eye.

Both of us were bleeding, but I was in my kitchen adrenaline rush and was not about to let the incident stop the service. Afterwards, I realized what I had done, and I was not very proud. My thoughtless action had risked the school's reputation and maybe even its existence. I could see the headlines of the local papers, "Chef assaults student – school closed!"

The following day Fran Voigt, the President, called us both

into his office. "So, Sam," he started, "tell me what happened last night with Chef Michel, and what should we do about it?"

As my career flashed in front of me, Sam said, "Nothing, Fran. I deserved it and that is the way we settle things in Alaska. May I be excused,? I have mise en place to do."

...

Fran, who often speaks in public, still tells this story, even taking some small liberties to make clear what it takes to have "the right stuff" in the kitchen.

Back at Yale with Julia Child, Long Wharf Theater, 1981

A Successful Life
4-oz portion

¼ oz education
¼ oz hard work
¼ oz modesty
¼ oz attitude
3 ounces of patience
Shake it well and add a zest of luck for a very successful life .

After the First Year

In June of 1981 I received a phone call from old friends from Connecticut, asking me if I would cook for a fundraising event featuring Julia Child at the Long Wharf Theater in New Haven. This was the menu I created for the occasion.

Ceviche de St. Jacques

Simi Chandon

La Selle D'Agneau aux Aromates

Les Primeurs du Vermont

Les Feuille de Laitue

Le Sorbet de Poire

Les Gourmandises

Moet & Chandon Brut Imperial

Café

Hennessy V.S.O.P. Cognac

The ingredients had to be transported to Vermont for prep, cooked in one of the kitchens at Yale, then delivered and served to 150 people at the Long Wharf Theater.

...

The dinner was a success, and the beginning of a long friendship with Julia. She came to New England Culinary Institute to be the graduation speaker in 1984. Her niece came to the school as a student in 1996. The school was getting to be known as the school "where you learn by doing."

In June 1982, a well-known Chicago chef, Louis Szatmary, asked me if I would like to enter "The Crab Cooking Olympics" in Baltimore. I had never entered a cooking contest, but it was an opportunity to bring recognition to New England Culinary

Institute. You had to make three dishes that included Maryland blue crab – a soup, an appetizer, and an entrée. I made a saffron blue crab soup, a terrine of blue crab with avocado sauce, and for the entrée, crab Americaine with Lobster sauce.

I brought Tim Corcoran with me, a second-year student who had done his internship at the Four Seasons in Philadelphia. We had to work out the logistics. We were assigned to use the kitchen of a restaurant on Baltimore's waterfront. The smallest pot they had was a five-gallon pot, which was problematic in the soup category. We did not win first place with our soup, but were pleased to win first places in the appetizer and entrée categories, not easy to do against the local chefs. By winning I was officially deemed "The Crab Master." Now, there is a title for you!

It felt good to be the little guys from an unknown school in Vermont beating the local big dogs. For me it was like being at the Academy Awards ceremony when I heard, *The winner is Michel LeBorgne!* Tim and I returned to Vermont, triumphant.

photo: Bob Willis

*Winning the Crab Cooking Contest
with Tim Corcoran, 1982*

The Tavern Motor Inn, the site of our main kitchen, was sold to a local lawyer and orthodontist, who had their own ideas about how to run a hotel restaurant. They knew as much about running a restaurant as I did about wiring teeth or drawing up a will.

Chef Michael Prevost was fast gaining a reputation in Montpelier for his great buffet and banquet work. One Saturday at the Tavern we were doing the wedding for the daughter of a well-known granite quarry owner. We were serving 250 people, including the lawyer, who felt compelled to contribute his two cents about how to run the wedding. He wanted a portable bar by the swimming pool, which was against state liquor regulations. When we told him that his response was, "This is my place and I do whatever I want." He wanted to push liquor at the wedding, because it was a cash bar. In the middle of the wedding, someone leaned against the bar, filled with liquor and ice, and it went into the pool, along with the cash box and several guests. Michael and I thought it was hilarious, although others did not.

With the school expanding, we had to come up with ideas of how to entertain the students on weekends, to give them an alternative to unsupervised drinking. We came up with the idea of a quadrathalon, with teams of four students each. We gave each team a mystery basket. One student had to bike five miles, then take the basket to the prep cook in the Tubbs kitchen, who wrote the menu and started the preparation. When the prep was done, the cook put the food on a sheet pan, and handed it to a runner who had to run uphill for one and a half miles to the school's Green Mountain Building.

Running uphill is already difficult, but imagine it carrying a sheet pan with food. The runner delivered the prepped food to another cook who actually cooked the meal according to the menu. Finally it is served to a panel of four judges who rate it according to presentation, taste, balance of ingredients, and timing. It was a nice way to spend a Sunday afternoon, followed by a picnic made by students.

The quadrathalon started getting very competitive, so we changed the rules slightly. Instead of making a mystery basket, we gave the students money to do their own shopping, giving them more opportunity to apply what they were learning about wine pairing, smart purchasing, and eliminating waste.

One Sunday four students – Scott, Clay, Jack, and Susan Jo – decided to take the money for their team and go to Stowe for a good time. I thought it was funny, because it was something I would have done at their age. Not everyone at the school agreed, but I loved those pirates. They always showed up at work on time and were very professional.

The quadrathalon started attracting TV and press coverage, because of the colorful way we were demonstrating cooking methods while incorporating physical fitness, which few cooking schools emphasize. Students arriving at New England Culinary Institute received passes to the local health club, and were asked what their fitness goals were for the semester. If they did not have a goal, we gave them one. It could be to lose weight or give up smoking or, as one student told me, to improve his sex life. We encouraged students to exercise to get rid of the embedded stress and frustration of the kitchen. It's better than sitting on the couch and polishing off a six-pack.

Next we invited other cooking schools to compete against us in the quadrathalon. It became an annual event, but lasted only five years, because no school could beat us. We had a great cyclist, Stephen, and a great runner in Alister, a former rugby player from New Zealand, who now owns a restaurant in Wellington named Logan and Brown. Another student, Marcella, a Dartmouth graduate, could do anything. Ahmed was Moroccan-born and came to the U.S. to play professional soccer but ended up at New England Culinary Institute pursuing a different dream. (He later represented the U.S. at the prestigious *Bocuse d'Or* in Lyon, France where he finished third and had the top-rated fish dish.) What a great group of students we had!

The school opened a new restaurant on Elm Street in Montpelier called Tubbs. This quickly became the place where people went to celebrate special occasions. I hired two chefs. One was Michel Martinet, a master of classic French cuisine who was notorious for having bad knives which he sharpened on the doorstep. To this day I have never met a chef who can cut anything as quickly and accurately, even with a bad knife, as Michel Martinet. I also hired Sam Sarakani, a native of Thailand, who did not talk very much but demanded discipline and silence. When students talked too much, he would turn off the exhaust fan in the kitchen, making it unbelievably hot. The students learned very quickly to cut down on their chatter.

Chef Patrick had apprenticed in France illegally and had great passion for the profession. He was a former welterweight boxer. One New Year's Eve day I was making lunch, and he was making dinner. I met his students in the parking lot as they arrived at 6:30 A.M. I called out to them "Hey you guys have come too early to do your mise en place," and they yelled back, "Oh no, Chef, we are just leaving." Chef Patrick had them working for a straight eighteen hours, through the night, to be ready for New Year's Eve. And they loved it!

We started to realize the two owners of the hotel were not keeping up their part of the contract by not paying us what they owed. This was a serious problem. We were a small school, still new, and we needed every penny. We had to make a quick decision. We could not close the school like you close a business, because we were obligated to the students who trusted us. On December 31st, after serving the last meal, around 2:00 A.M., we closed the kitchen, packed every pot and pan (which was not a lot), emptied the refrigerator, freezer, and storeroom, cleaned everything, and moved it all to a nearby space on Elm Street, a former take-out sandwich place called The Crust and Cauldron. It had a good reputation with the state employees in town. We changed the name to Elm Street Café. The students, in the midst of packing up, thought it was funny, because they loved giving the owners of the Tavern what they deserved. They also loved the drama. Everyone volunteered to work all night to move to our new location.

Another opening! Mon Dieu! After cleaning the place I took stock of the place we had moved into. There was a regular home electric stove, a home refrigerator and a walk-in. We worked all day Sunday, doing the mise en place, so we could open on Monday. We worked all day New Year's Day. We rewarded the students royally for their hard work, and everyone made the experience fun. It did not feel like work. Every year I get Christmas cards from these students, telling me that this was the best New Year's party they ever had.

On Monday we opened to the public, as if nothing had happened. We served sixty-eight customers the first day and put a special sandwich on the menu nicknamed "The Elmo." It was open faced, a slice of toast, mayonnaise, a layer of sliced Granny Smith apples, topped with melted Vermont cheddar cheese. This was served with a cup of soup, and for years was our best-selling item on the menu.

When we left the Tavern Motor Inn, we also lost classroom space, but by now our momentum and determination was so great that nothing was going to stop us. We arranged to hold classes in a local church. In America, where there's a will there's a way.

Elm Street Café became very popular. It was cozy with the tables very close. The wallpaper may have been peeling off the wall, but when you have good food and courteous service, people give you the benefit of the doubt.

One day Jeb Spaulding, the owner of WNCS Radio, which is now "The Point," called to ask if I was interested in doing a talk show. I agreed, and Steve Zind, who is now a fixture with Vermont Public Radio, was the host. The show was live. In the first half hour I would talk about a subject, perhaps roasting, and then people would call in with tips, recipes, and questions. Sometimes I had the answers, sometimes not, but I never faked it.

One day the subject of the radio show was cooking eggs, one of the most difficult things to do consistently. How many times have you received a chef's salad with hard-cooked eggs where the yolk was starting to turn green, because it is over-cooked? It is guaranteed to taste bad.

In 1984 New England Culinary Institute was commissioned to do the cake for the inauguration of President Reagan to take place the following January. The cake was to be an exact rep-lica of the Capitol and had to feed four thousand people! No small task! I do not remember how many eggs or how much sugar we used, but first we made a sponge cake and the butter cream icing in Vermont. We then trucked the cake and other ingredients to Washington, D.C. to be assembled. I was sick and could not be part of the final team, but I had fabulous students to carry on, students like Drew O'Keefe, who now owns a restaurant in Leesberg, Florida, and Bob Bennett, who later was the pastry chef at Le Bec Fin in Philadelphia and now owns a superb pastry shop in Cherry Hill, New Jersey named Miel. That is just to name a few. They worked forty-eight hours straight to decorate this cake, making it into a work of art. They finished fifteen minutes before the public arrived. Who says timing isn't everything!

With Fran Voigt, Howard Fisher, and John Dranow, 1986

After several years of having our Montpelier domicile be the "home away from home" for several flights of students, we decided to get a little privacy for ourselves by buying an old farmhouse in Northfield, one town to the south. It needed some repairs, but I didn't mind, because I thought this is where I was going to retire. We had land where we could snowshoe in winter and hike in the summer. It was a peaceful place where I could recharge my batteries on weekends … until, that is, the students discovered that our little piece of heaven could be theirs, too. Let the non-stop wine, cheese, and cooking classes (without grades) begin! It may sound like I am complaining, but it was great fun, too. The only time when the crowd became smaller was when there were leaves to rake or wood to stack. How did they know?

In the summer of 1986 Anne-Marie and I went to Napa Valley to visit some of our graduates. This was a dramatic and tangible proof of the fruits of my labor. We had lunch – a very long lunch – at Domaine Chandon, where the kitchen was mostly staffed with New England Culinary Institute graduates. Danny Michaud was sous chef, and the brigade included John Dowman, Sara Erickson, Sharon Feldman, Leah Cohen, Doug Weldon and Bob Melioris. It was like a class reunion! We spent the afternoon drinking sparkling wine and taking trips down memory lane.

Domaine Chandon is owned by Moët and Chandon, a champagne company in Reims, France. Champagne can officially be made only in the region that bears its name. Anywhere else, including Domaine Chandon, it must be called sparkling wine. Domaine Chandon has a beautiful restaurant with a large terrace in the middle of the vineyard in Yountville, California. The chef, Phillipe Jeanty, treated us like visiting royalty. To see my students doing well and showing off their talents in a restaurant and vineyard of high repute gave me a sense of serving a purpose on this planet.

The following night we had dinner in San Francisco with René Verdon, the chef of the White House under Kennedy. René offered to sponsor me to become a Maître Cuisiniers de France, the highest honor to which a chef can aspire. There are 350 chefs in the world with this title. You do not earn the title by taking an exam, but rather by being recognized by your peers for your accomplishments. I soon found another sponsor in Robert Greault, the owner of La Colline in Washington, D.C.

The code of the Maître Cuisiniers de France was written in their charter in 1951:

I. *The Master Chef of France must be aware that he belongs to a renowned cultural tradition.*

II. *As heir to a great past, his mission is to serve the culinary art by expanding its influence and providing for the future.*

III. *Versatile by nature, he must not only be an excellent cook but also a high-level restaurant keeper.*

IV. *His professional technique must attain the level of high art.*

V. *For the Master Chef of France, his scrupulous regard for his culinary principles excludes neither professional development nor the individual creative spirit needed to express his personality.*

VI. *His first step in this approach is to select the best products and to strive constantly for perfection.*

VII. *The Master Chef of France lives in his kitchen and so makes sure that his workplace is clean, pleasant, and functional, by observing the principles of hygiene. In this way, he can ensure harmonious relations within his team and, in turn, efficient work.*

VIII. *A Master Chef of France must run his establishment with a permanent concern for cleanliness and comfort.*

IX. *The Master Chef of France must manage his guests as potential friends, whatever their position, standing, or amount of the bill.*

X. *He must guarantee the good quality of his services without neglecting the smallest details and concerns, as befits a fine restaurant.*

XI. *In our time, the Master Chef of France has become a prominent personality, and in certain situations, he may be required to act as an ambassador of his Association, thus implying continuous personal efforts to advance professionally.*

XII. *In view of the moral weight of his title, a Master Chef of France enjoys a certain degree of independence, even though the opinion of the media is a reference that cannot be ignored.*

In June of 1988 I was inducted into the Maître Cuisiniers de France in a ceremony in New York City. My membership was to recognize both my cooking skills and the accomplishment of opening a cooking school. Membership in the organization included Paul Bocuse, Jean Trois Gros and Georges Blanc, so it is an understatement to say I was proud to be in the company of these professionals. I allowed myself only two glasses of champagne that night, because with all the excitement and emotion, I was already feeling tipsy.

The school continued to grow and in 1988 opened a branch in Essex Junction, Vermont, in a brand new inn called The Inn at Essex. We contracted with the owner to run two restaurants, a fine dining establishment called Butler's for the students' senior year training, and a brasserie bistro, called the Tavern. We also had a fabulous facility with bakeshop, pastry shop, and even a meat fabrication facility where our chefs taught sausage making and butchering.

I recruited Chef Robert Barral from the Four Seasons in Boston. He had previously opened a few resorts for the Four Seasons. The school was now in good hands. We quickly gained the reputation as being the place to go for seminars and conferences – and great weddings!

As the school expanded, we needed more students. I started recruiting nationwide, doing demonstrations, TV appearances, and attending open houses with alumni. Traveling, eating airport food, and living from a suitcase are not fun, however. I was always happy to come back to Vermont and to teaching, because that is where I find my greatest rewards.

Maître Cuisiniers de France

130

Our Training Ground

Tubbs Restaurant was in a very nice, brick building that had once been the city jail! Tubbs was always my favorite restaurant for teaching. One reason was the scale. We averaged forty-five to fifty for lunch, just enough to get busy but not too crazy. The most lunches we ever did was 103, during fall foliage. This statistic was provided by Patrick, my faithful pot washer. I never met anyone so proud of his job, and I never had pots and pans so spotless. He was my MVP! Every three weeks, when we rotated the students, I introduced Patrick as the pot washer *formidable*, and I gave a lecture to the students about the value of a good pot washer. *It is very simple. If one of you guys is sick or doesn't show up, I have no problem taking over your station. Even two stations. But if Patrick doesn't show up, I am dead, because I have no one to wash my pots.* It was from my training with Chef Bernard that I learned the importance of the dishwasher.

Patrick never missed a day. We let him eat whatever he wanted on the menu whenever he wanted. I told the students up front that if they burned the pots, they would have to scour them clean themselves. This was not part of Patrick's job.

We had three special customers who ate at the Tubbs bar every day – Ken Merrill, Hugh Weedon, and Klaus Falkenraft. They were connoisseurs, real gourmets, and they kept me on my toes! They were well-traveled food lovers connoisseurs who would try anything, except Mr. Merrill, who had posted a "barf list" of foods he did not like, including zucchini, broccoli, fennel, beets, peppers, onions, turnip, cauliflower, brussel sprouts, artichoke bottoms, cabbage, and olives. All three loved Dover sole, but also loved a good eight-ounce hamburger. This was a challenge, because students have a tendency not to pay as much attention to a hamburger as an expensive filet mignon. I always taught: *You must learn how to cook a hamburger per-*

fectly before you cook a veal chop or a filet mignon. Also you will make a lot more money selling hamburgers. Now, it is chic to add foie gras to the burger. It is delicious. Fat is flavor!

Once a week during the fall and winter, I made a *cassoulet*, a French classic. Basically, it is baked beans with lamb and pork, duck confit and garlic sausage, baked very slowly for hours. The dish became so popular that Tubbs customers brought in their own casserole dish to take it home. Occasionally I made other sauces for customers to use at home. Mr. Merrill's favorite was truffle sauce.

Returning second-year students always presented a challenge. We'd joke they had come back for a second beating. By now they were dedicated, with a passion for the industry. Some, however, thought they knew everything, because they had now worked in some very good restaurants. Since this was their last year, I had to make sure they knew not only about cooking, but also how to be mentally fit for working in a real-world kitchen environment.

Every morning we had breakfast together. The students took turns cooking. While we were eating, we talked about baseball and football, or news events, and then food. I never gave lots of homework. They only had two things to do for me. Every day they had to read and find something I did not know or that I had never heard about food. This was a great exercise. It did not take them too long not to look for French classics.

Through one of these exercises, I learned about Panko, which is Japanese bread crumbs made from unleavened bread. Everyone learned and benefited, plus it was fun. Also, they had to come with a new dish for the last two days of the academic block. The criteria were no truffles, no foie gras, 30% food cost, seasonal availability, and customer appeal. The final day of the block was my treat. Steak and eggs and grits.

Here's a practical test I gave the students. I doled out the same amount of butter, onions, leeks, potatoes, and water to everyone. Salt was on the table. Their task: make a potato leek soup. If I had six students, I got six different soups. That is when you find out if people really can cook! I was always taking notes, and could tell you who was going to be a good cook,

132

though I could not always predict who was going to be a good chef. A good cook is someone who can cook very well in all styles. A good chef is not necessarily a good cook but a good business person who surrounds himself or herself with good cooks. This is an important distinction, because in this country there are lots of good chefs who know how to make money and are surrounded by very good cooks. They themselves are not necessarily good cooks. I could name you a few, but I won't. The good cooks in this world do not necessarily become the TV stars.

Among other hats the chef must wear: purchasing agent, inventory control clerk, menu creator and writer, taking into account customer preferences and seasonal availability, and public relations agent to promote the restaurant (or, in my case, school). He or she must also be very handy, so the chef can fix things with some troubleshooting. For instance when the ice maker stops, most people call the repairman, who will charge you a minimum of $80. For $80 he probably will remove the front panel and push the reset button. You also must be a good psychologist to find out what makes your employees tick and be able to work well with others.

A list of my successful students would be too long, but I can promise you that every one made a very good potato leek soup.

At our last meal together, we played a game where my students had to reveal their fantasy meal – that is, what would they like to eat, drink, where, with whom, and listening to what music. There were some funny ones. Charley wanted roast beef on rye in a New Hampshire brewery with his dog, listening to Charlie Daniels. Steve wanted a clambake with all the Dallas Cowboy cheerleaders, listening to the Rolling Stones. They always wanted to know my fantasy meal, so here it is – Belon oysters, rye bread made by my father-in-law, washed down with a bottle of Muscadet on a little beach in Brittany watching the sunset to a backdrop of John Lennon singing "Imagine." Now you know everything about me.

Before the students left, I gave each one an oral evaluation so they would not agonize waiting for the written evaluation.

Then I always asked, "What do you see yourself doing in five or ten years?" Some simply said, "*I dunno, Chef.*" That's the same answer I would have given back in 1957. One blond kid from Atlanta told me, "Chef, I am going to have my own TV show." Well, his name is Alton Brown, and he probably has the best show on the *Food Channel*, called "Good Eats." Hats off to you, Alton!

Another student, Eric Johnson, a very funny kid, said, "Chef, I am going to be a rock star." Eric had everything planned. He worked three years for Daniel Boulud in New York City at Daniel's, then four years for Jean Georges Vongeritchen at Jean Georges, who has twenty-two restaurants worldwide. He gave two months' notice to Jean Georges, telling him he was going to Thailand, just as Jean Georges had years earlier.

A month later Jean Georges told him, "You are going to open a restaurant for me in Paris."

"But Chef," said Eric, "I don't speak French."

Jean Georges said, "Yes, but you can cook, so learn French fast!"

He opened Marche in the Sotheby building on Avenue Matignon in Paris, with a one and a half million dollar kitchen. In opening the restaurant Eric worked ten straight weeks without a day off. The restaurant had twenty-two reviews, twenty-one were excellent and one merely good. Eric was upset about that! Try to imagine the challenge to a young American chef! I'm glad we helped prepare him for that.

One night we went to Marche for dinner. Erin, Rachel (both New England Culinary Institute graduates), Anne-Marie, and I. Needless to say we had a fabulous dinner. The most amusing part of the evening was that people around us wanted to know who we were. This is a place to be seen – famous models, clothes designers, jewelry designers, la crème de la crème, so we must be important people. When the service was over, Eric came out and sat down. I asked him how his French was coming along.

"Well, people understand me."

"Eric, I know your teacher."

"How do you know?"

"Isn't it the hostess? She's the most beautiful one in this room."

He blushed. "Oh Chef, you are funny."

Two years later we were going to have dinner together during the Paris Food Show. When I called to confirm, someone told me he had returned unexpectedly to New York. I became worried and when I returned to the states, I called Jean Georges's office only to find out that Eric was on his way to Shanghai to open another restaurant for Jean Georges. Eric, you are a rock star!

Another outstanding student was Joung Shone. Korean born, she had been enrolled in law school in Chicago, but her passion was cooking. Coming to NECI made her the black sheep of her family, but she was an exceptional student, extraordinarily self-disciplined. She spent both of her internships at the Everest Room in Chicago with Jean Joho. We called each other once in a while to see how things were going. One day she said "Chef Michel, Joho said he is going to take care of me. And he said, stick with me." Although she was getting more and more responsibility, her paycheck was not getting any bigger. I told her, "If Joho said he will take care of you, he will take care of you."

Several months later I was in Las Vegas where Joho was recruiting to open the Eiffel Tower restaurant, a half-size replica of the famous monument. Joung and I had dinner at Picasso, one of the best restaurants in the Bellagio complex where the paintings are all originals by the master. The meal was as good as the artwork. Joung and I talked business. of course. Chef Joho was in the process of hiring a new chef, to be trained by Joung for the first month. By chance I happened to see this guy's car. It was filthy, the ashtray overflowing with cigarette butts, I knew that this guy would not work out for Joho. He lasted two weeks, after which Joung Shone became executive chef at the Eiffel Tower, a position she still holds! Take my word that her paycheck has gotten bigger.

One night I was her guest, seated at the best table overlooking at The Bellagio. Suddenly, I had tears in my eyes, because I realized I am the richest man in the world. I say no crying in the kitchen, but that does not apply to tears of joy.

When I teach I emphasize the importance of uniformity of cuts, knife skills, and control of heat and seasoning. And patience! You have to be quick, but you cannot rush good food. In the early days at NECI we had a three-to-one ratio of male to female students, but the top students were frequently women. My theory is that this is because the female students know they are entering a man's world where the odds are against them. To compensate they try harder. In general women are better listeners and neater, a very important characteristic in the kitchen. They question your authority less and are, therefore, easier to teach. The ones who really excel, from my experience, are ones who also have experience with team sports. They know how to be part of a team, and to take instruction from a coach. As athletes they are better coordinated and have more stamina than their non-athletic counterparts.

Team sports have a similar importance for male students. Many real achievers have learned perseverance from their experiences on the field. And it may be my imagination, but I find they drink less, perhaps due to their physical training. Of course, as with all generalizations, there are always exceptions.

La Brioche

La Brioche was our bake shop located in the same building as Tubbs. We had a talented, but crazy, French pastry chef named Thierry. He had trouble understanding why he could not smoke his *Gauloises* while baking or order drinks at the bar at lunch. This was not in the teachers' handbook! Chef Thierry was a great teacher, but he enjoyed the night life, and Montpelier was not Paris.

One morning when I arrived at work, I went to the bakeshop to say my customary hello to Chef Thierry and the students. I could not believe my eyes. Someone had knocked down the metal, fireproof door to get into the bakeshop. The students were in there making pastry, croissant, brioche, and bread as if nothing had happened. I asked what happened to the door. They responded that the night before they had gone to Stowe with Chef Thierry, who had too good a time. The students brought him back to Montpelier and put him to bed. The next morning they arrived at the bakeshop knowing Chef Thierry would not be in working condition. No one had a key, so Bruce, a well-built guy, did the next best thing. He knocked down the door so that the croissants would be ready on time! You had to admire their dedication! Unfortunately, Bruce had to pay for destroying the door, but everyone else chipped in.

In 1996 we closed Tubbs and Elm Street Café. We consolidated the menus of the restaurants and reopened on Main Street in the location of my former competition, The Lobster Pot. 117 Main Street Grill was on the ground floor and basement, with the more upscale Chef's Table on the second floor. I had mixed emotions when I served the last meal at Tubbs. I was sad to be leaving a place that held so many fond memories of teaching and working. Restaurants promote intensely strong connections with staff, students, and customers. It becomes like a family with a highly demanding relationships and experiences that can provoke strong emotions. At times you feel like screaming or crying if things are not going your way. The pace and pressure are constant and require that you keep many things in your brain at one time. Your success is dependent upon the others in the kitchen. But there are great times, too, with joking, laughter, and the joys of human connection. Leaving the family can be hard. Luckily, with Tubbs my sadness was tempered by the excitement of opening a new restaurant.

Many customers came to the kitchen to thank me. It was the end of a great era, twelve action-packed years. But time to move on. One can't afford to be too sentimental. There is only one thing to count on in life, and that is change.

A chef in a small restaurant in a small town like Montpelier has both the pleasure and opportunity to meet customers. Some become friends. You get to know their likes and dislikes; you run into them at the Saturday farmer's market. (People always watched what I was buying, wondering what I am going to do with it.) Occasionally I'd be asked for a recipe, which I usually wrote on a brown bag or on the back of an envelope. I also would add my phone number in case they encountered problems. You would be amazed at how many Saturday afternoons I was invited to dinner by my customers. Knife skills were a problem for some of these amateur cooks. People did not realize how dull their knives were. I taught some classes on Saturday nights with my customers at their homes. The proper cooking and carving of a turkey was the most frequent request. It was fun teaching with a glass of wine in your hand!

And, by the way, Montpelier is the only state capital where you will not find a McDonald's, a Burger King or Wendy's. That bit of trivia is good for a free beer in any bar in the U.S.!

The school was getting such a widespread reputation that the Department of Tourism of Costa Rica wanted us to open a school in their capital, San Jose. Fran Voigt, the President, and Gary Janson, the Vice President, made several trips to negotiate the contract and to look at their existing facility. Everything was moving along until Chef Robert Barral and I went down to Costa Rica for one week to do demonstrations and to participate in the Food Show of the Americas. Here we were, two French guys representing North America!

It was an eye opener – the culture, the poverty, the lack of sanitation.

We met chefs from another culture, something I love. I met a Cuban chef, Gilbert Smith, an interesting gentleman who spoke French and English fluently. He had once been the chef at the Cuban embassy in Paris, and we discovered that we had several common acquaintances. Before the Cuban revolution in 1959, he had been the private chef for Meyer Lansky, the notorious gangster. Lansky offered Gilbert the chance to go back to the States at the time of the revolution, but he decided to stay in Cuba.

I also met a young energetic French chef, Gerard Germain, who was a chef at Los Tahibos in Santa Cruz, Bolivia. This was the beginning of a friendship that would help me discover South America in years to come.

On the business side, however, my instincts told me it would be very challenging to open a school in San Jose, Costa Rica. I expressed my concerns and reservations to Fran and NECI never did open the school.

Potato Leek Soup

Serves 4

Prep time: 15 minutes

Cooking time: 25 minutes

The Story

Leeks must be one of the most popular vegetables in France; you can eat them au gratin, or cold with vinaigrette. They are easy to grow and they will last the winter even if the ground is frozen. Fifty years ago every cook knew how to make this soup; now it is another story, they prefer to go to a take out! Even in France the eating habits have changed, and not for the better.

The Recipe

1 oz butter
1 large onion, diced fine
1 leek, sliced thin
Salt
1 qt cold water
1 large potato, diced small
Salt, pepper
½ C heavy cream

Clean the leek; hold by the roots and quarter lengthwise. Run under water to remove any dirt. Melt the butter, add onion, leek, and salt and cook slowly until the onion and leek are tender, then add the cold water and potato, cook rapidly until the potato is tender. Check seasoning. Put the soup through a blender, half of the container at a time. Add the cream while blending.

Note: this soup can be served cold; add chives and you have a vichyssoise.

NECI Commons

In the summer of 1997 I had back surgery. Taking care of the property in Northfield became a serious problem. I am not the kind of person to hire someone to do my work. We decided to move to Burlington. Anne-Marie officially retired from anesthesia and the school to step back and enjoy life. She deserved some reward after all her hard work!

In August of 1998 we opened NECI Commons on Church Street in Burlington. This was to be the flagship restaurant of the school. Another opening! I thought Elm Street Café was my last one! Chef Robert Barral did this opening with me. Two heads are better than one! First we had a "soft opening" where we tested recipes before the restaurant was open to the public. The food was served to the wait staff so they would be familiar with dishes and better able to describe them to the customers. In too many restaurants the wait staff has never tasted the food.

The restaurant had two floors. Downstairs we had takeout and pastry, a brick pizza oven and rotisserie. The kitchen had a large window so that the public could watch chefs and students. I like open kitchens. The staff is more conscientious about working neatly, not talking loudly, keeping uniforms clean, and maintaining a professional bearing. There were seven stations, plus the rotisserie and brick pizza oven, which was run by a paid employee, Abraham, who was a great pizza maker, computer geek and showman. NECI Commons, located on Burlington's pedestrian mall, Church Street, was an instant success.

Success is not rocket science; it has a simple formula. You buy the very best; you handle it properly; you cook with love; and you serve with a smile. Know your clientele. A good location helps. At NECI Commons, we were successful every day even with student apprentices who only stayed with us for only two weeks before moving to the next block of instruction. Every day – rain, shine, or snow – we opened at 11:30. My friends in the industry say it is impossible to maintain high standards with students cooking, but it is not that hard when you love what you are doing and convey that to the students. Most importantly, you must embrace the KISS (keep it simple, stupid) principle. We did an average of 200 lunches and 250 dinners. I never did drugs, but I swear I was high on an adrenaline rush, especially at service time. Any chef knows what I mean.

For me, it is like conducting the Boston Symphony, doing a dramatic piece of music from Bartók. Maybe I did not have a first violin, but I had an apprentice. I was the conductor, the expediter who calls out the orders spit out by the computer. *Ordering and fire, two calamaris, one goat cheese, one crab cake.* Overseeing the students was my most important job.

Some of the apprentices were unforgettable. I remember one who would just look at me and by her expression and body language, I knew whether or not she had gotten the order. It was magic. *Ordering two cods, one stroganoff.* Another student was a little slower, so I had to change my intonation and timing to get him up to speed. Always, it is critical to give students ample time to prepare dishes.

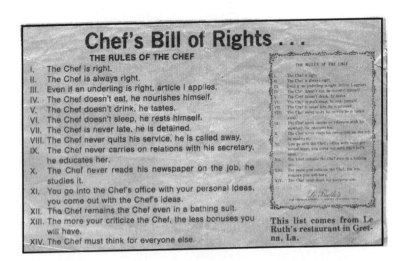

Chef's Bill of Rights . . .
THE RULES OF THE CHEF

I.   The Chef is right.
II.   The Chef is always right.
III.   Even if an underling is right, article I applies.
IV.   The Chef doesn't eat, he nourishes himself.
V.   The Chef doesn't drink, he tastes.
VI.   The Chef doesn't sleep, he rests himself.
VII.   The Chef is never late, he is detained.
VIII. The Chef never quits his service, he is called away.
IX.   The Chef never carries on relations with his secretary, he educates her.
X.   The Chef never reads his newspaper on the job, he studies it.
XI.   You go into the Chef's office with your personal ideas, you come out with the Chef's ideas.
XII.   The Chef remains the Chef even in a bathing suit.
XIII. The more your criticize the Chef, the less bonuses you will have.
XIV.   The Chef must think for everyone else.

This list comes from Le Ruth's restaurant in Gretna, La.

The View from the Kitchen – Latin American Travels

MEXICO

By the mid-1990s the New England Culinary Institute had established a reputation as one of the best cooking schools in the country, with a growing roster of graduates spreading its gospel to the far reaches of the food world. Increasingly, this resulted in opportunities for travel and teaching in other countries I was only too glad to accept.

Two New England Culinary Institute graduates, Jessica Delaney and Benito Molina, invited me to be the guest chef for a special Valentine's Dinner in Ensenada on the Baja Peninsula of California, two hours south of San Diego. Manuel Trevino was an intern and Jessica was a chef in a restaurant called Las Esquinas. Benito was a chef in a restaurant at a vineyard known as Santa Tomas. I was invited to be the guest chef for Valentine's Day. This dinner I was to be guest chef for and were sold out. Jessica and Benito picked me up at the San Diego airport and drove me through Tijuana to buy several bottles of tequila. During prohibition the famous Caesar Salad was invented here, named for its inventor, Caesar, who was maître d' at a Mexican casino. We drove on down the coast and stopped in a restaurant to eat fried lobster. My first reaction was, what a waste, but it was not that bad, especially when washed down by a cold Corona, even though I would have preferred a boiled lobster with melted butter. The restaurant was near the site where the movie, *Titanic* was filmed. Yes, they made icebergs in Mexico!

We finally arrived at the vineyard Santo Tomas. The wonderful vineyards of Baja California – Casa de Piedra, Adobe Guadelupe, Monte Xanic – seem like an extension of Napa Valley. Chateau Cannon even makes great tequila that had been aged in an oak casks that once held sherry.

We were served superb Mexican food by the kitchen crew.

Benito invited the whole staff to a tequila tasting with Cohiba cigars handed around. I have never been a tequila aficionado, and I gave up up cigar smoking when I was eight years old. My father made me smoke a homemade cigar, because an old lady who lived nearby squealed on me when she saw me smoking a cigarette behind the church. We always did things behind the church, thinking we were close enough to the church that God would protect us, but this time it had not worked. I had been smoking with my two friends, Claude and Bernard, and my father made me smoke the whole cigar which he himself rolled. I turned green, I turned purple, and I got very sick for two days. Probably this was the best lesson my father taught me because I never smoked. Unfortunately, he died of cancer from smoking two packs a day.

But back to our tequila tasting! We tasted six to eight glasses, and we got very serious about the tasting. We started with a brand that is very popular in the U.S., followed by a better grade of tequila – no lime, no salt – a real tasting like the tasting of wine or cognac, but no spitting! Then we got into tequila that was to my liking. It was a great education again, to find out tequila that is available in the states is not the very best that is available in Mexico. Now I have acquired some knowledge about tequila. Unfortunately, the one to my liking is very hard to find in the states, and it costs mucho dolares.

The following day was devoted to the mise en place for the Valentine's dinner. Everything went according to my planning before the kitchen crew left. I told them that I expected everyone to be in the kitchen by 10:00 A.M.

On Valentine's Day I was on deck at nine o'clock, one hour ahead, just to be comfortable and familiar with the kitchen. By ten o'clock there was nobody there. 10:30, nobody. Eleven o'clock, nobody. 11:30, nobody. I panicked and ran across the street to see Jessica, who was chef at Las Esquinas.

"Jessica, it's 11:30 and nobody is here. What is going on?"

"Chef Michel, this is Mexico."

"But Jessica, we have 150 reservations."

"Chef, have an espresso and relax."

"But Jessica…"

"Don't worry if you are not ready at 8 or 8:30! Then you open at nine!"

"What?"

"Don't worry, Chef Michel, nobody will show up for dinner before nine o'clock this evening."

The kitchen staff was made up of three people, and they showed up at 12:30 in a pink truck. They called out to me, "Hey, Chef Michel, let's have lunch. We will cook for you." I replied, "No, no," and they told me they were going for a fish taco. At that time I was exhausted from worry, so I decided if you can't beat them, join them. They took me to the pier for a delicious fish taco. Meanwhile it was two o'clock and no sign of Benito. I got ticked. *Slow down, Chef Michel.* Those three guys and Chef Memo, started the mise en place by three o'clock. What a relief it was to see those guys working like lightning. Precise. Clean. Smiling. It was amazing. The mise en place was done in half the time I had scheduled for it. We then sampled every dish before service.

One of the dishes was an abalone ceviche with the local lime. The abalone was local, small, tender and very delicious. Then we had a warm potato salad, truffles and lobster. The potatoes had to be the same size and cooked with the skin on, then peeled hot and sliced the same thickness, then sauced with lukewarm vinaigrette. The lobster tails were also sliced with the same uniformity and between each one I put a slice of truffle. When service started, with Benito expediting, I just had to relax and watch. I wished I had the money to send those guys to New England Culinary Institute. They would have been such a good addition to the culinary world because of their work ethic.

Benito, Jessica, Memo and I went to Baja's oldest bar, which had once been a brothel, Café Husson, to listen to a mariachi band and drink tequila. Only the best for me, and when you drink the best, you do not get a hangover. I was in heaven meeting the guys who supplied the abalone, the butchers, and all the rest. Most of them had been educated at American colleges. Those people really knew how to have a good time and do business at the same time. This was the beginning of a long relationship I had with the local people and other vineyards.

The following year I was invited back to Mexico for a fundraiser for an orphanage in Ensenada during the *vendimia*, the vintage, grape harvest time, about the first week of August. For one week the local vineyards take turns fundraising by providing great entertainment, food and wine. Each vineyard does something different. There is local food and music. You buy a ticket and they were selective about who they invited.

The last day was the biggest fundraiser, held at the vineyard owned by an American, Dan Miller and his wife, Tru. To this day, I do not speak espagnol, but Tru, who is Dutch by birth, speaks ten languages. They have a beautiful estate in the Guadelupe valley. It is an expensive bed and breakfast with a large stable. The architecture is remarkable, designed to be a replica of an Iranian mansion. Also, it was designed so that the sun never bears directly down on the house. At noon the breeze would start blowing from the ocean through the courtyard. Even in the middle of the day in this hot valley, the house was never uncomfortable, but they also had air conditioning. I have been

*Fundraising in Ensenada, Baja California (Mexico),
with Manuel Trevino and Benito Molina, 1999*

in charge of the closing gala every year since then. I do not do it for money, but it is a lot of fun and sometimes frustrating, because I love the Latin life but find Mexican Time hard to adapt to!

One year I put Benito in charge of the dessert, which was a Roasted Peach with a crème Anglaise and a cold raspberry coulis. It was no big deal. As usual, I started early to have my mise en place ready one hour before. That year I had to roast rack of veal in a wood-fired oven. This was yet another learning experience for me.

I was also serving a risotto with *huitlacoche*, also known as the white truffle. It is a fungus from the corn. One o'clock came and no Benito. I called his apartment. Solange, his girlfriend, now his wife, answered the phone. "Don't worry, Chef Michel, Benito will be right over!" Guess what, when I called, the peaches were still in the tree, ripening . Don't ask me how Solange managed to get Benito there, but we had the dessert ready on time. Thank God the Mexicans eat late. By now I have learned how to work with the local people and enjoy life a little more. After all, there is always mañana!

BOLIVIA

With NECI Commons on automatic pilot, Chef Robert and I could attend culinary events in South America. Our first trip was to Santa Cruz, Bolivia. We were the guests of Gerard Germain, the French chef we had met in Costa Rica. It was my first trip to South America. I spoke kitchen Spanish, which is not much. Despite that, when I travel I am always eager to see how the natives live, eat, and shop. This is why I always go to the local food market – to me, this is where you get the feel of a country. I love to take pictures, and the market in Santa Cruz was one of the most colorful ones I have ever seen. Most of the produce was organic, but there was no refrigeration for the meat. You can buy a bag of coca leaves there, just like a head of lettuce.

The taxicabs were the first thing that attracted my attention. All of them are pre-owned Japanese cars. So they have the dashboard with the speedometer, rpm, and gas level indicator on the right side, but the steering wheel is on the left, just like in the States, but nothing is connected! Once when I was with Gerard, he asked the driver to show him the bags that the driver had under his seat. One was coca leaves, and the other one was baking soda. They make a mixture and chew this, like people chew tobacco. Those guys get a serious buzz and they can drive twenty-four hours, with their eyes wide open!

The last day of the Food Expo there was a big reception for us so we could meet the Santa Cruz dignitaries. Most of them had been educated in Switzerland, and they all spoke French and English fluently. They knew more about the restaurants in Paris and New York City than I did! That night I think I made a faux pas. We were talking about where Che Guevara was assassinated and how he was assassinated. My version was not their version. You could feel the strain this put on the conversation. Perhaps I should have steered clear of this topic, but I had walked into it, unaware of the unseen minefield.

We were never paid for our labor but we were rewarded with a trip to Lake Titicaca in Bolivia, which has an elevation of 12,000 feet. After the food show, we flew back to La Paz . Then we went to the lake on the bus. This was about a five-hour bus ride. I did not expect to see snow-capped peaks in South America. Our guide told us that it was good skiing. "How do you know about skiing?" I asked. "I was born in Austria, my father was a GI, and my mother was a native Bolivian," he told me. Not only could he ski, he spoke French, German, Spanish, and English.

Remember, this is the highest lake in the world, positioned at a very high altitude. We took a boat ride, and on the other side of the lake there were ruins of cemeteries in the hillside, and we were immediately surrounded by native kids who seemed to come out of nowhere because no housing was within sight. They were curious about us, and my Argentinean friend, Marianna, sang songs with them. They had walked from behind the mountain, probably about five miles.

ECUADOR

In 2002, Chef Robert and I were invited to a Food Expo in Quito, Ecuador. We had our work cut out for us between a TV appearance and a TV demo, and doing our mise en place for the final buffet at the end of the Expo. The mise en place was for both hot and cold dishes. I think Chef Robert and I worked very well together. He is a fabulous garde manger, and I prefer the hot food. For the buffet I made my signature dish, lobster hash, and some squab braised with cabbage and foie gras. I had the help of local students, and my Spanish was getting better. It was rewarding to work with these underprivileged kids from the area because you could see in their eyes how eager they were to learn. I will never forget a young lady, Cristina, and how anxious she was to learn from us. Now Cristina and I e-mail. She e-mails me in French, and I e-mail back to her in Spanish. I want to mention here that the attitude there towards women in the kitchen is not the same as it is here, and a woman in the kitchen does not get much respect. The result is that a woman has to work much harder to become a cook or chef, just as it was in America forty-five years ago.

As I mentioned, we never got paid, but we were always rewarded with a trip. This time we were to go to the Galapagos Islands, which I had been reading about since my childhood. The wildlife was everything and more than I had expected, including the giant turtles, and I went swimming with the sea lions. The natives care deeply about the environment because it is so fragile. It is so fragile because it is right under the equator and is very dry. If you step on a plant, it could take years for it to grow back. Jacques Cousteau and his son did a lot of research on the shores of these islands. What I remember the most is how good the food is, especially the fruit. It was there that I ate the best sorbet I have ever had, which proved my theory that you must start with the best and freshest of ingredients. They would literally pick the fruit right from the tree, that is how fresh it was.

We also took in the dance scene. The Latinos barely hear the music start, and they jump up to dance. They do not drink alcohol, instead they drink water or Coke, and right up until the music stops, they are dancing their hearts out. No union band over there!

URUGUAY

Two weeks after I returned from my trip to Ecuador, I received a call from the manager at the Sheraton at Montevideo, Uruguay. The manager was from Northfield, Vermont, and had eaten several times at the New England Culinary Institute. He had an offer for me to do something, and he told me that money was no object, I could get anything I want. When someone tells me that I am still conservative in planning the menu, I can write the greatest menu, but if, at the last minute, I cannot get my order, I am sunk. This is another opportunity for me to refer to my motto, the KISS (keep-it-simple-stupid) method!

He needed someone to introduce American cuisine to Uruguay. First I asked him what he thought of as "American cuisine." After a long pause, he said, "Well, what do you think it is?" There is no simple answer to this because American cuisine is a melting pot cuisine, just as America is made up of people who immigrated to this country from all parts of the world.

I did not think he would like lasagna, for all the respect I have for the Italian cuisine, or some bastardized chop suey, which, by the way, is an American invention. So I decided to do original American dishes, starting with New England of course. I did a New England clam chowder, again, my signature dish of lobster hash, scrod with lentils and roasted shallots, venison with cranberry relish, Indian pudding. Then I did Southwest cuisine from Louisiana and Texas – gumbo, crayfish etouffée, barbecued pulled pork and barbecued beef, jalapeño cornbread, enchiladas and fried okra and green tomatoes, and a pecan tart. Here are the menus.

New England Cuisine

New England Clam Chowder

Lobster Hash (my signature dish)

Scrod with Lentils and Roasted Shallots

Venison with Cranberry Relish

Indian Pudding

Southwest Cuisine from Louisiana and Texas
BBQ Brisket
BBQ Pulled Pork
Gumbo
Crayfish
Jalapeño Cornbread
Fried Okra with Green Tomatoes
Pecan Tart

California Cuisine
Avocado Salad
Abalone Ceviche
Cioppino *San Francisco Style*
Veal Medallion with Rappini & Polenta
Trio of Sorbet

Northwest California Cuisine
Oysters Rockefeller
Roasted Halibut with Stuffed Morels
Saddle of Lamb with Assorted Beans

Peach Crisp

The menu items we were going to serve buffet style, which is not really what I like, but they knew the clientele better than I did. After several days of email, I got in touch with the other chef, who, to my relief, was French. As it turned out, this was not worthy of relief. *Au contraire.* After assessing the work load in the kitchen, which I would have to share with other cooks, I decided to bring someone else with me. I selected a second-year student, Shannon Peach, who was American-born but had lived in Costa Rica for many years and of course spoke Spanish fluently. I asked her if she would like to come to South America with me for this event, and she said, "No problem, chef." On the way to Montevideo, we got delayed in Chicago, so we arrived in Buenos Aires late the following day. We missed our connection to Montevideo, so we had to stay overnight in Buenos Aires. That is where I called Marianna, the young Argentinean chef I knew, and we met for breakfast the following day. This was a completely unexpected chance to visit, and she offered to show us Buenos Aires on our way back. She did not have to twist my arm!

So we arrived thirty-six hours late in Montevideo. We had a problem in customs, and they confiscated our pecans. We had to go to work immediately, since we were so late. The pleasures of traveling! A brand-new kitchen, but, as usual, the kitchen was poorly designed. What do you think about architects who design a kitchen for a two-hundred-room hotel and a banquet facility for four hundred, but with only one oven in the kitchen, and one in the pastry shop? Do you think they would have enough brains to talk to a chef who has been in the business for twenty-five or fifty years? Architects do not understand the work flow or the traffic in the kitchen. Because of this, they do not know how to make the kitchen functional.

All the cooks were very nice to us, they wanted all our recipes. In the States we are trained to be ready to serve at 6:00 P.M., but the cooks in the cafeteria were relaxed and reading newspapers at 6:00. I talked to Shannon and asked her what was going on and she replied, "Chef, nobody eats before 10:00." So she quickly updated me on the South American living style. After a couple of days we knew where everything was in the kitchen. I was astonished by the quality of the produce. Everything was organic with a lot of dirt, which is a good sign of its freshness, and everything was delivered in color-coded plastic crates, everything was returnable. No throwaway cardboard boxes like in the States.

Every morning one of the cooks came and picked us up and took us to Montevideo. And every day we ate in the market or a local restaurant, except one day Shannon needed a fix of a Subway sandwich. If you love meat of any kind, you must go to Uruguay or Argentina. They have huge wood-fired barbecues called *parilla*. When it comes to meat, you name it, they have it. Chicken, pork, beef, sausage, kidney, and the portions are huge. All served with French fries, no salad or vegetables. The meat is so good because all is from free-range animals. They are leaner, a little tougher, but much tastier. What most people have for lunch is a plate of French fries, lots of meat, a pack of Marlboros and a beer. It did not take us long to get used to the lifestyle, minus the Marlboros!

Almost every night one of the cooks would invite us to share dinner with their families, and then all of us went to the famous tango bars. They are unique, because not only can they tango, many people get up and take turns singing with the band. It was startling to see people singing with such passion. The bars would not close until 7:00 in the morning. At the bars they serve you a drink called *medio medio*, which is half cognac and half champagne. In size Uruguay is like a small Switzerland, and I would love to return there. It would be hard not to love the people of Uruguay because of their warmth and openness.

On our way back to Buenos Aires, we took a two-hour ferry across the Plata River, and Marianna was there to welcome us. After we got used to the pollution and the way they drove, everything was great. For our first lunch Marianna took us to a typical restaurant where you only eat meat. You help yourself to a salad bar, then the waiter comes to your table holding a large skewer and slices your meat, as much as you want. Everyone has a disk on the table – green on one side and red on the other. When the waiter finishes serving you, he puts on the red side. If you want more, you turn it on the green side. They give very attentive service, and if you need more meat, you turn the disk on the green side. Then they will immediately come to your table and give you the serving of your liking. Again, the meat was excellent, not our standard U.S. meat, certainly leaner and with more taste.

We visited the famous cemetery called La Regolato with the mausoleums where the dead are buried, which are overrun with cats. For reasons I do not know, people feed the cats in the cemeteries. Visiting a cemetery is like visiting a museum because of the carvings in the mausoleums. We also visited Casa Rosa, where the Perons lived. Montevideo looks as if it were designed like Paris – very sophisticated with its broad avenues and stylish shops. We also visited La Boca, the poor neighborhood. It was both very colorful and very poor. Even though it was the poor section, it was very clean and colorful with window boxes. It was also where people tango down the street, just to entertain the crowd, who throw them money.

PERU

The following year, a Latin American cooking organization called the Aregala Association invited us to Lima, Peru, for the Food Expo. It was summer in the States, but it was winter in Lima, which consists of three months that are very foggy, months you do not see the sun. We were guests of Gabriela and Alfonso, who owned three seafood restaurants in Lima. One night we were invited by the Japanese community to have sushi and sashimi with them and share the Japanese culture. The sushi was memorable, as well as their hospitality. There is a large Japanese community in Lima. On the streets there are natives who walk around the avenue with change. They make change for the tourists who have American money, and they give you a better rate than the bank will.

After three days of our cooking demos, food displays and preparation of "American" food, using local ingredients, the people came to taste the food. American food was going to be put to the test! Preparation was hard under such rugged conditions, including no running water, and we had to improvise constantly. Here is where my apprenticeship training helped, because fifty years before I had been trained only with basic equipment and conditions, so I had learned how to make do and be creative with what we had. What was remarkable was that there were always people in the kitchen who wanted to help us, because they also wanted to learn from us. We had the American flag flying over us, but they seemed more interested in the food because we were French. And you better believe my Spanish got better! This time, at the end of the Food Expo, we were rewarded with a trip to Machu Picchu.

We flew to Cuzco, where we spent the day visiting Inca ruins and architecture and the market. The corn sold by the street vendors particularly astounded me. Never have I seen corn with kernels so big! Vendors were selling artichoke bottoms. First they would cut off the leaves at lightning speed, and the bottoms are tournée. They chose to cook the bottoms because they are more tender and flavorful than the leaves are.

I never knew about potatoes and Peru. At one time Peru had four hundred different kinds of potatoes, long before the Irish. The dehydrated potatoes sold in the market fascinated me. The farmers, without any machines, dehydrated them. They would put the potatoes on the roofs of their houses, and the potatoes did not rot. This was because the altitude and the sun would naturally dehydrate them. I can not explain it better than this, because that is all I was told. The Inca Indians probably discovered this trick a long time ago. You can buy dehydrated potatoes by the bag at the market, which are also a lot lighter to carry home too!

We spent a day touring around Cuzco, visiting incredible cathedrals. When the Spanish invaded South America, they destroyed almost all of the Inca temples and robbed the sites of all their gold. However, several years ago when there was an earthquake and these structures were damaged, the Spanish-owned telephone company paid for their restoration, in some way trying to restore some of what had been taken hundreds of years before.

Chef Robert and I shared a room, and we learned to take quick showers because the water was heated by the solar panels. The following day we took a very basic train to go to the base of the canyon, which is the base of Machu Picchu. As we got closer, I became more and more excited. It was almost overpowering – the landscape, the people, their colorful clothes, the big sky. From there we took a bus, which brought us up to Machu Picchu, where we were greeted by the barefoot children who wanted to sell us something. At the top we got out and looked down at Machu Picchu. After seeing it only on postcards or in magazines, it took my breath away. There is a spot on Machu Picchu where people go to meditate, with the mountains all around them, where they say you can feel the energy. And you can feel the energy. No one actually knows how the stone buildings were built, some say the stones were rolled up the mountain on tree logs. It is something of great wonder and mystery.

We went back down the mountain and at the bottom we looked up into the night sky. I have never seen so many stars. This is because there were no lights anywhere nearby, and the altitude makes the air very clear and unpolluted.

Educating a Village

Before we opened New England Culinary Institute (NECI) in 1980, I was interviewed in New Haven by the owner of the Tavern Motor Inn on State Street in Montpelier, Vermont. The school did not have a kitchen, and Fran Voigt, the President, thought the kitchen of the Tavern would be a perfect training ground. The owner, a Mr. Avery, however, did not trust the inexperienced Fran to run his kitchen. He wanted to talk to me directly. He asked me to describe an example of a good meal. After some reflecting, I said, "braised pot roast and potato." Touchdown! This was what the legislators and the locals wanted. Now, we had a kitchen.

Two weeks after the school opened I met Alan LePage at the Farmer's Market, then located on Elm Street, next to the courthouse. It was June. Vendors were selling jam, brownies, honey, and maple syrup. There was the interesting "Spider Man" who was mounting spider webs on wood . Another guy was selling Vermont walking canes. Alan LePage was the only organic farmer. He is a very interesting guy who passionately believes in what he is doing. I decided to take my class once a week to his farm. It was enlightening for the class and a good refresher course for me. Students learned why an organic carrot costs more than one in the plastic bag at the supermarket. One day, Alan took the students to the field and showed them how to weed the carrots. They quickly realized that kitchen work is easy on your back compared to farming.

I tell students to learn to cook using only salt and fresh herbs. One day we picked carrots, washed them, cut them uniformly, and put them in a pot with very little water, butter and salt. The pot was covered and the carrots slowly cooked for twenty minutes. I added freshly chopped parsley, also from Alan's farm. For some students this was the first time they had eaten carrots that were not drowned in water, brown sugar, and maple syrup. The carrots actually tasted like ... carrots.

Alan started to deliver his beautiful produce to NECI. At the beginning, we had a little problem. Alan would show up with crates and crates of butter and oak leaf lettuce. As good as the produce was the local Rotary Club wanted only iceberg wedges with orange French dressing. *Yuck!* Out went the salad bar with its croutons, bacon bits, and twelve different dressings. We started serving real salads, lightly tossed with oil and vinegar, but also well presented. Still I never refused French, Long Island, or Russian dressings since the customer must always be pleased. I started to write my specials with seasonal vegetables. But I still couldn't take all Alan's lettuce, and he couldn't understand why.

One afternoon I went to the farm. We walked through the fields of his labor of love, and I explained how kitchens function and how my business is as unpredictable as the farmer's. This informal meeting was the seed of chef-farmer collaboration which is now the Vermont Fresh Network. Fried chicken morphed into coq au vin, or sautéed chicken breast with side salad. The square fish covered with sawdust, deep fried, then slathered with tartar sauce was eliminated in favor of broiled swordfish or sautéed salmon with beurre blanc. No more canned clam chowder (even though I admit some canned chowders are pretty good).

All dishes were to be made with fresh vegetables and water rather than chicken base or stock. I changed the club sandwich recipe, offering cranberry jelly as an alternative to mayonnaise. I was wary of going too fast in terms of changing the eating habits of Vermonters. The customers made the choice of cranberry jelly or mayonnaise. Pot roast was reintroduced as braised beef with local vegetables and was an instant hit.

Another interesting character in Montpelier at that time was Jules Rabin, the bread maker from Plainfield. He built a wood-fired oven that was available to the community after he baked his fabulous sourdough bread. Plainfield was not quite ready for this, especially during mud season. I could live on his bread alone. Jules was making deliveries twice a week of two dozen loaves of sourdough bread in a flour bag. Jules was recycling ahead of his time.

The bread basket we were serving at the time consisted of sourdough bread, a roll, and a muffin. People rarely touched the sourdough so I turned it into the real French toast, and they loved it. No more soggy, spongy toast. I made bread pudding and excellent garlic croutons. Gradually, the students converted to eating Jules' chewy, but delicious bread.

One day a young lady walked into the kitchen and introduced herself in perfect French. *"Bonjour, Chef Michel. Je suis Allison Reisner* (now Hooper) *et je fabrique des fromage de chèvre."* This was heaven ... goat cheese for my sour dough bread. Allison had learned cheesemaking in France and now had a small goat farm in Brookfield. Her business, the Vermont Butter and Cheese Company, has now won scores of national awards and has spearheaded a renaissance in artisan cheesemaking in the state. She would stop and give me samples of her new cheeses, all of which were superb. I remember her boursin, tom de savoie, and an incredible marscapone.

I served her cheese with fruits, nuts and Jules' bread. This was 1981. In 18 months while teaching the basics to six students, I was slowly transforming the eating habits of hundreds of Vermonters.

There is a great butter from The Vermont Butter and Cheese Company. One cheese, Constant Bliss, is from Jasper Hill Farm. Lazy Lady Farm makes a Valençay chèvre. Great Hill blue is made from raw milk, and there is a marvelous cheddar that is aged for four years from Grafton, Vermont.

Last, but certainly not least, our daily bread from my friend, Gerard Rubaud, from Fairfax, Vermont, who built his own wood-fired oven and who insisted on organic wheat to mill his own flour. That is a labor of love, and oh, what a great bread! Once in a while I drove to his little paradise to share a bottle of wine, paired with paté spread on his beautiful bread. Now, that is living!

A typical menu for the day was:

Black Bean Soup

Spinach Leek and Salsify Soup

Smoked Trout and Sour Cream Omelet

Linguini with Shrimp Chili Sauce

Pan Fried Scrod with Artichoke

Sautéed Scallops with Endive

Sautéed Lamb with Red Curry Sauce

Pork Tenderloin with Rum Orange Sauce

Veal Medallion with Spinach and Prosciutto

Sweetbread in Lobster Sauce
(I had mixed reaction about this one, but it proved more popular than calves' liver. To this day I still can't sell calves' liver.)

...

In reflecting on culinary Montpelier in the early 1980s, I can't forget the Grand Union, the local grocery store. The produce choice was iceberg lettuce, spinach, carrots, celery, and potatoes. The wine selection was half gallons of Carlo Rossi Almaden, Mateus (in a green, pear-shaped bottle), Cold Duck, Wild Irish Rose and maybe a couple of French and German wines like Blue Nun. That was it. One day I was shopping and bought fresh spinach. When I got to the cashier, she asked me what it was. I answered, "spinach." She replied, "Oh, I thought spinach only came frozen." We have come a long way, baby!

I also met Danny Cox, who had just founded Green Mountain Coffee Roasters. It is remarkable that Ben & Jerry's, Vermont Butter and Cheese, Green Mountain Coffee Roasters, and NECI all opened their doors in 1980. Together we have changed the eating and drinking habits of Vermont.

Entertaining The Maîtres des Cuisinier de France

In June 1999 the school hosted the annual meeting and dinner of the Maîtres des Cuisinier de France. What an honor, but also what stress, to have your peers coming from France to little Vermont. The night before we had a clambake on the shores of Lake Champlain. Most of the guests had never been to a clambake. We served Magic Hat beer, donated by the local brewery. The sunset over the lake was spectacular that evening. For most of the guests, who thought of the United States as a combination of New York City and Hollywood, this was an entirely different and thoroughly enjoyable American experience.

We had 120 guests. Julia Child was the guest of honor. She was elected La Dame de l'Année by l'Academie Culinaire de France. Andre Soltner, one of the most famous French chefs and the former owner of Lutece in New York, and the French

Maîtres des Cuisinier de France Gala at Inn at Essex with Julia Child, 1996

consul from Boston were there. From the French consul I received Chevalier de l'Ordre Merite Agricole from the French government. In translation this means "Knight of the Farm"! This is given in recognition of the promotion of the French culture and gastronomy. Louis Pasteur also received it because he invented pasteurization. I was pleased to be in such good company!

Most of the members of the Maîtres de Cuisiniers de France and their wives attended. We also invited the mayor of Burlington, Peter Clavelle. Many famous chefs from Paris were there. It was a big success. For that I have to thank all the students and chefs at New England Culinary Institute who helped pull it off.

The dinner menu was lobster hash, roast rack of veal with spinach and blue cheese polenta, a grapefruit campari sorbet, local salad with all Vermont cheeses, hot chocolate bombe and petit fours.

At the end, the pastry chef had made a replica of the medal of the Maître Cuisinier of France, mounted on a chocolate pyramid. I told the guests, "One of you at each table will take one home with you." There was one for each of the twelve tables. They had to turn over their coffee cups, and the ones with green dots on the bottom could each take one home.

What Goes Around, Comes Around

In 1954, when I started my apprenticeship at the age of fifteen, I learned to make espagnole sauce, a foundation sauce made with a brown *roux*, brown stock, fresh tomato, mushrooms, mirepoix of carrots, onions, thyme, and bay leaves. From this we made a demi-glace, which is an espagnole sauce reduced to perfection. Somewhere along the line someone eliminated the brown roux and replaced it with arrowroot to make the sauce lighter. Now, we just reduce the brown stock made from veal bones. Some chefs roast them, some do not. The changing approaches to espagnole sauce provide a good example of how cooking has evolved during my lifetime.

A second example is béchamel, another mother sauce, originally made with a roux moistened with milk, then baked in the oven for several hours. This was delicious. Today, béchamel is made quickly. Some chefs do not even make béchamel and, instead, use a reduced heavy cream. Done properly, it tastes very good. (For macaroni and cheese dishes, however, I recommend sticking with the traditional.)

When I was an apprentice, the cuisine was called *La Grande Cuisine Bourgeoisie*, and all the cooking was done "whole." For example, you would roast the whole chicken, which would then be sliced or de-boned in the dining room. This was a period of very generous portions, and sometimes second servings.

Next came Service à l'Anglaise in which the tray or platter of food is set up in the kitchen, then placed on a table, served by very skilled waiters.

For the past twenty-five years we have been in the period of *La Nouvelle Cuisine* in which the plate itself is set up in the kitchen, with calibrated portions. Seconds? Don't be ridiculous. Originally, as with all new trends, La Nouvelle Cuisine was criticized by traditionalists, but now is accepted.

I treasure my copy of *Le Repertoire de la Cuisine*, purchased when I started my apprenticeship in September of 1954. It is the Bible for any chef. I also have my *Travaux Practiques de Cuisine* for learning cooking basics. In 1980 when we opened NECI, I used those same textbooks and in twenty-five years those same books will be in the library of any cooking school.

When I graduated in 1957, I bought *L'Art Culinary Français* by Ali, Bab, E. Duval, A. Escoffier, P. Montagne, and H.P. Pellapat. Most of the dishes are classic, with hearty sauces, presented in silver trays or finished tableside.

These books were created at a time when a kitchen brigade had 10-12 people. It walks you through the various stations – soups, eggs, fish, meat, poultry, but also sauté, pan fried, roasted, and sauces. By mastering the basics and adding a little creativity, you can create an infinite number of new dishes.

When we trained, we made dishes from Alsace, Provence, and Normandy. Each province's cooking is influenced by the weather, geography, and seasonality. France, smaller than Texas, has so many unique cuisines which have become classics for the world.

Normandy is on the English Channel. It is a green, luscious land and its proximity to the sea means access to a wide range of seafood – sole, turbot, oysters, mussels, and so much more. *Sole Dieppoise* is a poached Dover sole with a white wine sauce, garnished with shrimp and mussels. *Á la Normande* usually means heavy cream, butter, apple, cider, calvados (apple brandy), and a cheese such as camembert. Brittany, also a coastal province, has many seafood dishes, including such classics as lobster a l'Americaine and langouste en Bellevue.

The Loire Valley is known for its salmon, shad and shad roe, and beurre blanc. It is where the famous sauce was developed, making use of the native grey shallots and muscadet. The southwest region of Perigord gives us truffles, foie gras, and cassoulet, a classic that combines the food of two civilizations. Arab influences with the lamb and beans are matched with the duck confit and garlic sausage from the local tradition.

Pays Basque is known for their tuna, sardines, anchovies, sheep cheese and pepper, such a *piment d'espelette*. Many books have been written about the cooking in Provence which is strongly influenced by nearby Italy and the Mediterranean climate. Aioli, bouillabaisse, ratatouille, ravioli, the burgundy, the greatest pinot noir, the boeuf bourguignon, crayfish, pike quenelle, poulet de Bresse – all trace their origins to Provence.

Alsace is another great wine district, whose cuisine incorporates German influences, featuring items such as charcuterie, sausage, venison, and eel.

...

As I contemplate what was accomplished in this country for the past twenty-five years, I wonder what we are going to be in the next twenty-five years. Ten years ago I predicted Las Vegas would be the most trendy food town in the U.S. Not a bad bet for a beginner?

Yet I do not have a crystal ball. Cooking is like painting, fashion and music. We still play Beethoven and Mozart, and I think we will play the Beatles as classics twenty-five years from now. Just like Elvis Presley, the Beatles are classic, here to stay. Fashion has Coco Chanel and St. Laurent, also classic designers. Because of Chanel's simple but distinctive design, I can now recognize a Chanel suit walking down the street, whether in Paris or New York. (You do not see a lot of them in Vermont.) In the world of art, we have Van Gogh, Pissaro, and Gaugin. In cuisine we have classics: cassoulet, dover sole meunière, a perfect roasted poulet de Bresse. And what about really great barbecued spareribs? They are here to stay. Oh, I almost forget to mention the pastrami sandwiches at Katz's in New York!

Looking forward I can see another twist to the cuisine and the service. Future cuisine will be served more efficiently and with more variety. Joël Robuchon is spearheading what will become the norm in Haute Cuisine. Assiette Degustation already exists with new china, shorter menus, and simple presentations at his restaurants in Paris, New York, and Las Vegas. An example is Scallop Degustation, where you receive three individual scallops, served on appropriate small china and cooked differently. The goal is to amplify the flavors, not to hide them. This is less time consuming, because you don't play with the food and it may be, ultimately, less expensive. I like this method, because is only a great technician will succeed.

One day my friend, Chef Jose Gutierrez, who apprenticed under Paul Bocuse, was instructing my students on making mashed potatoes. Easy? No, because first you have to peel a potato properly. Ridiculous? Not in my eyes. I will say more about potatoes very soon.

Paul Bocuse is probably the chef who had the biggest influence on some of the changes in the culinary world. Thanks to him, chefs are now recognized as professionals, not servants. We do not enter the establishment where we are working by the back door with the garbage, but by the front door, just like the customers do. In the mid-1990s the fad was to build up the food like the Eiffel Tower! Bocuse called this "the erection cuisine." It did not last too long!

Others who promoted important changes in the culinary world were Julia Child, James Beard, and Jacques Pepin, each of whom, through the world of television, entered our homes and made cooking accessible to everyone. Before this, there was the concept that what professional chefs did to prepare a menu item was different from what we could do in our kitchens. These three also taught us that cooking can be adventurous and fun, and Julia, especially, let it be known that she made mistakes in the kitchen too!

I told you I had more to say about potatoes! Joël Robuchon made mashed potatoes a noble dish. When he was in Paris, you needed to book your reservations for his restaurant Jamin two months in advance. I was told that some people postponed their operations to have a table there during the 1990's. You did not expect to be served mashed potatoes in a restaurant of this caliber. This is why I give him so much credit. He made a noble dish and received the accolades of le tout Paris. There is no secret to this, just buy the best and cook it well.

The potatoes he used are called *ratte*. They look like golden finger potatoes. First they are washed and cooked, skin and all, in salted water. When done, they are drained and then dried in the oven, then peeled, rapidly of course. Put them through a sieve to avoid working the gluten, and also so there will be no lumps. Then place the pot on the fire, stirring with a wooden spoon, preferably made out of olive wood, because the olive wood does not crack or absorb water. Then you must incorporate chunks of cold butter. Finish off with boiling milk to give a silken texture. Try it. It is to die for!

Andre Soltner, the chef-owner of Lutece in New York City, dazzled three generations with his *basse en croute*, a bass wrapped in a striped bass mousse and baked in a crust. It is a very difficult classic because you have three different textures. The bass must be cooked to perfection, the mousse should not be rubbery, and the crust must be flaky. The dish was on the menu every day until Lutece closed.

Jean Georges Vongerichten, after being trained classically in France, worked in Singapore, Bankok, and Hong Kong. He is the only chef, in my view, who understands "the Fusion Cuisine." This is because he has lived, worked and eaten in France and Asia. Fusion is a very delicate balance of flavor, texture, ingredients of two continents. Fusion Cuisine is not simply adding lemon grass, ginger and *nuoc man* (Vietnamese fish sauce) to a chicken broth and calling it a Vietnamese soup.

Michel Guerard started *Cuisine Minceur*, which literally means "slim cuisine," because he was concerned about the health problems and obesity of the general public. Made with fresh local produce, his superb dishes, served in smaller portions, sacrificed neither flavor nor taste. This was not a diet of celery and carrot sticks!

Daniel Boulud never forgot his roots in Lyon, France, where eating is taken very seriously. But he certainly adapted his food to fit the sophisticated tastes of New York City at his restaurant DB.

Alice Waters, on the West Coast, certainly was a pioneer in this nation because she simplified the menu and insisted on using local, seasonal, and organic food. She continues her mission by educating and improving the eating habits of school children and promoting sustainable agriculture at the same time. I wish her daughter had been at Yale when I was there. Now Alice Waters is educating the Ivy League about food!

...

Thanks to people like Julia Child the profession of chef has become a source of celebrity. Many cooks have written books, some good and not so good. How many recipes do you need for béchamel? The culinary planet has gotten smaller. In the U.S. we are now strongly influenced by chefs from Japan, Vietnam, Thailand, Mexico, France, Italy, and Spain. Unfortunately, China never let great its best chefs emigrate to the U.S. and, in my opinion, Chinese cuisine has not improved comparatively with other countries.

Trends and fads come and go – blackened fish, the short cooking method, small reduction. We are constantly discovering new foods and cooking techniques – croissants, arugula, cilantro, balsamic vinegar, flavored oil, coffees of all descriptions, panini, the sushi bar, and organic food. It is now officially "cool" to go to cooking school. The *Food Channel* opens the door for edible circus acts and still more gimmicks. Celebrity chefs are everywhere. For some, watching Emeril is like watching a soap opera, but overall, any attention is good for the industry. Unfortunately, the *Food Channel* can't tell you if the food is good and how hot it is in the kitchen.

More serious from my perspective is that in America the length of the meal is not well managed.

The public wants more gimmicks, whether undercooked green beans or more undercooked fish. This is why chefs must adapt to the present without forgetting the principles of tantalizing the palate. You need to seduce customers with new dishes and pique their curiosity to come back to your restaurant. Years ago I thought we would be serving veal cheeks, beef cheeks, rare tuna, and cheese trays. It made my day, recently, to learn that Alain Ducasse, one of the most celebrated chefs in the world, is opening a brasserie in New York City at the location of La Potinière where I worked in 1964. He is serving cassoulet, veal blanquette, beef bourguignon, and tarte tatin, the same dishes with which I started my career!

One more time, what is good remains! Except, that is, when the "good" is on the plate. Then, it disappears very quickly.

…

As much as the classics stay the same, change is constantly occurring. The French classics have been reinvented and made lighter, thanks to pioneers like Michel Guérard. Joël Robuchon went to Japan to teach French cuisine, but he also learned there about lighter presentations and the immense technical improvements to be made by simply cutting ingredients. As I said, he turned mashed potatoes into a noble dish and has the accolades to prove it. Andre Soltner, the chef/owner of Lutece in New York City, dazzled three generations with his bass en croute.

Opening a Restaurant

At New England Culinary Institute there is not one week that goes by without our receiving a call or letter from someone who wants to open a restaurant. But there is a lot to consider before going into the restaurant business, which has the highest rate of bankruptcy of any business sector in the U.S. Six out of nine restaurants do not make it through the first six months. There was a TV show, *Restaurant*, which portrays how difficult it is to run a restaurant. So the question for me is, Why do so many people who have no background or experience in the food industry want to open a restaurant? I love to drive fast cars, but I am not going to buy a gas station or a garage.

From my perspective, there are different categories of people wanting to go into the restaurant business yet who are unlikely to succeed in this business. There are the foodies who think – because they love to go out and eat in places where it is cool to be seen – that they will buy a restaurant and impress their rich friends. A friend of mine, Marcel, opened a restaurant in L.A. with several partners, but Marcel was the only one who knew how to run a restaurant. The restaurant was an instant success. The partners were eating there every night with their guests. Two months after the opening the partners wanted to reserve two tables every night, just in case they decided to come for dinner, or one of their friends wanted a table.

This did not last too long, because Marcel told them they would have to pay for eight people every night, regardless of who showed up. This is an example I use of some people's lack of understanding of how the business works. You must plan on so many tables with a certain turnover. That is what makes the restaurant money, not just the quality of the food or the atmosphere. The partners had not thought about this from a business point of view, but Marcel made sure that they did think about it.

There is another category, these dreamers who think it is a glamorous profession. It may be for a few, but you have to make lots of sacrifices, and nobody comes and takes my picture on a Saturday night after service, which is a good thing because I do not look so good!

Still another category: In some of the affluent New York suburbs, you have lots of women who entertain lavishly, so their friends might say, Suzy, you are such a good cook, you should open your own restaurant. Suzy's husband is a big gun on Wall Street, but he is getting ready for a change. So they jump into the SUV with two teenagers, headed to Vermont during fall foliage. Oh, darling, don't you think it will be great to run away from the big city, the crime and the rat race and raise our two children in beautiful, peaceful, safe Vermont? And so they buy a bed and breakfast. Six months later they may be broke, may be ready to divorce, inclined to drink more. There are a few exceptions to this, but you do need to know that you will need a large fortune to make a small fortune.

And then there are those who only go out on Saturday night, when restaurants are always full. You can hear them complaining how much they paid for their filet mignon, because they think they can buy the whole cow for that price. But they are forgetting about the overhead and the taxes, not to mention theft and breakage. They also assume that their restaurant will always be so busy. These ones usually last about two months.

On the other hand, there are some very successful chefs, like Jean Georges Vongerichten and Daniel Boulud, in New York and Las Vegas, Wolfgang Puck in Los Angeles and Jean Joho from Chicago. These chefs have built an empire, not only because they are good chefs but also because they are good businessmen.

Their background and mine are the same. We are all immigrants who came here with our knives and a suitcase or two, who set out in a new country with the desire to succeed. Another thing we have in common is that we were all trained by great chefs who drilled the basic cooking methods and the discipline of the profession into us. We all knew we would have to pay our dues, and we did not expect instant success, like the new generation does. Let me assure you, this is not a business for those who want immediate gratification.

Here is the key. You start small, take care of your employees, take care of your customers, do not hang out in night clubs every night, and avoid the police blotter. You do these things, and some day someone will offer you the chance to become a partner with them.

How these guys can run so many restaurants – that can be the grind of this business.

Consistency is the name of the game, and these chef-owners always promote from within the company. Line your ducks up and watch your pennies if you want to be a chef and own a restaurant!

Jean Joho – or Joho as we call him – owns The Everest Room on LaSalle Street in Chicago, in the financial district, and Brasserie Jo in Boston, near the Prudential. He also owns The Eiffel Tower in Las Vegas, whose chef, Joung Shone, is a New England Culinary Institute graduate.

And then there are the diner owners, and diners are an important part of the history of food in America and American culture.

Finally, the smartest ones of all are the ones who own two hot dog stands, one in Maine and one in Florida!

I am proud of my accomplishments, but most of all that I had the opportunity to educate a generation of clinicians, chefs, managers, bakers, pastry chefs, wine store owners, cheese makers, beer makers, teachers, even a TV star with his own cooking show. Because of this I consider myself the richest man in the world. I have tried to pass along my love and passion for this great profession to another generation. Not only have I had the opportunity to teach cooking but also to teach self-discipline and working hard. I tried to encourage and coach students. This is the reward that I have had that I never envisioned, which has been an unexpected gift in my life. I hope this book and my stories will help the entrepreneurs, and all the others, to know what it takes to put a meal on the table and keep you smiling!

Teaching the Next Generation

In 1996 I was voted Chef of the Year by the Maître Cuisiniers de France. The reception was held at Citrus in Los Angeles, where my friend Michel Richard was a chef. I also received the Medaille de la Ville de Paris. It is a medal given by the mayor of Paris to French ex-patriots who represent French culture with honor. Still, my greatest honor was the privilege of teaching.

Teaching is both the most exasperating, but also the most satisfying, profession. Teaching others to do things properly is much tougher than doing it yourself. At NECI, students have no choice but to jump in; this is the definition of hands-on training. A student has no opportunity to hide in the back row, praying not to be noticed. Different students learn things differently, and at different paces, and the teacher has to adjust accordingly. Teaching is an especially rewarding profession when you, the teacher, see the impact on a student of something you have taught. Sometimes when I watch Alton Brown on *Good Eats* I will glimpse something that he picked up from his days at NECI.

Like bad restaurants, mediocre cooking schools will self-destruct, and only the very best will survive.

We opened the New England Culinary Institute on June 1, 1980 in Montpelier, Vermont. Twenty-five years later we are told that NECI is certainly the best culinary school in the nation. Our reputation among the professionals in the industry is very strong because of the unique training we give the students. The International Association of Culinary Professionals awarded NECI their 2004 Vocational Cooking School of the Year award. And when the chef of Per Se in New York is a NECI grad, you know that the on-the-line training has succeeded in bringing out the best in the best.

Some students have more self-confidence than others, but that doesn't predict who will succeed. The quick learners may have talent but burn out. Those who are slower have to try harder, and sometimes their tenacity will lead them to success. You do have to be well-coordinated to succeed in the kitchen; that is the nature of the beast.

Younger students can be very vulnerable. The lure of alcohol or drugs is very strong, and there are notoriously high rates of addiction in the culinary profession and in the restaurant business in general. At the other end of the spectrum some students come to NECI without a direction in life and after several weeks, their eyes sparkle with interest. That's when I know they are hooked, and are consumed by the adrenaline rush that comes when movement and skill are combined. Some students' feet hurt the moment they put their shoes on. They usually get a quick refund.

After twenty-five years of teaching the culinary arts, I know a lot of people in a lot of places. Many students stay in touch and invite me to the establishments where they are cooking or even the properties they now own. I can go to almost any city and have students to call. I rarely dine alone and thoroughly enjoy looking in on their lives. Anne-Marie and I also receive invitations to weddings. We try to attend as many weddings as possible, because weddings are so joyful and fun. These connections keep my world from shrinking. I am flattered that three students have named their children Michel, and one even named her dog after me!

There is a NECI saying that "Shiny shoes are happy shoes." It is a joke, but a reference to my requirement that students wear impeccable uniforms and shiny shoes. I want students to take pride in their work and profession. Anyone who has a problem with shiny shoes gets a quick return trip to the dorm to shine their shoes. On such mornings I was not the most popular chef, but now we all laugh about it.

If I had strictly stayed in the food service business by working in or running restaurants, I would not have had such a rich and interesting life. Students made my life interesting by challenging me with questions, many that I had to research before answering. I am constantly learning and still try to stay abreast of new developments and phenomena in the culinary arts. As I get older there is a tendency to cling to the familiar classics, but I continually remind myself that the classics are always evolving. Who thought when the mop-headed boys came on the *Ed Sullivan Show* and played "I Want To Hold Your Hand" that years later world-class orchestras would perform Beatles classics? What is good remains.

The Service

One thing I would like to see in this country is better table service. Now it is not considered a profession, it is something you do to make extra money when you go to college. Until the day the people will start tipping 2% for bad service, instead of leaving 15% or 20%, we will continue to get bad service.

John Mariani, the food writer and book author, once told me, "In this country if you are average looking with all your front teeth, you can make $50,000 a year waiting on tables." Maybe you're not a straight A student or you didn't go to college, but you can always wait on tables. I also know many bright college graduates waiting on tables, because it is easy money. Personally, I think it is a difficult profession.

In Europe waiting on tables is a profession that you learn in school (like cook, lawyer, or banker). As with all professions, there are good ones and bad ones. In the United States, however, waiting on tables is a condition, something you do between jobs, to support yourself while going to college, or to moonlight after your regular nine-to-five job.

In France you have to go to school for three years to become a service professional. First you are taught to walk properly with grace, like a ballet dancer. Then students learn table manners. You are instructed on how to converse with the customer (more than the, "Hi folks my name is JJ and I will be your waiter tonight" common in this country). There is also instruction in foreign languages. Most staff at a high-end restaurant in France speak three languages. In the U.S., I do not know too many bilingual wait staff. Those who speak Spanish typically do not speak English.

Tableside service, although not often practiced any more, is still taught. It was a relief to chefs when it became acceptable to set up plates in the kitchen. This is food delivery, not service.

A professional server also learns cooking, wine, cheese, and food pairing, as well as menu writing and management, because the goal is to eventually become a maitre d' or a restaurant manager. With the exception of the top-of-the-line restaurants in this country, very few wait staff are so well-rounded.

After graduation the aspiring server chooses the type of restaurant to work in. Not everybody can work at the Lucas Carton or Robuchon. Some will choose brasseries and bistros, but all have in common the tuxedo, the black vest, white apron, and no ring in the nose. Hair must be short and only mustaches are allowed. In the U.S. it is the restaurant owner who sets the rules. Standards vary widely. Some wait staff are very professional and impeccably dressed, others just throw a polyester jacket on their back. There are places where you see staff in blue jeans and sneakers. It is hard to know the difference between customers and wait staff.

In France, 15% is added to your bill regardless of the service, plus wait staff expect a tip. I don't like the system. In U.S., you give whatever you want. Americans tend to be too generous and tip 15% regardless of the service . Some establishments even give you a little card to help you calculate 15%, 18%, or 20% of your bill. I do not tip on taxes. I do have a soft spot for the sixty-year-old diner waitress who gets up every day at 5 A.M. and smiles as she hands me my coffee. She makes my day and on a $10 breakfast, I always give a $3 tip.

People tend to tip according to the food quality, good or bad. Tipping, however, should not reflect the food, but the service. The waiter did not cook your meal. On the contrary, if the food is not to your liking and the waiter offers to replace it, take it off the bill, or offers you a free dessert that is good service. A good waiter wants you to leave happy. I still have a problem with the waiter chewing gum, walking to my table singing. I can tell he is a frustrated artist.

How many times have you had this experience? "Hi folks, I'm Johnny. Where are you folks coming from? So, are you having dinner with us this evening? Anyone care for drinks?" By this time I know my evening is going to be ruined. I am going to watch every single move, and, at the end of the meal, tell him what he did wrong and leave a tip that is the equivalent of minimum wage.

He proceeds to tell us the specials of the evening. Although it is 8:30 P.M., he still reads them from his little note pad, clueless of what those dishes are and how they are cooked. Example: "The scrod is sautéed in white wine." Think about it. After his five-minute recitation, he asks us if we are ready to order. Since we are not, he disappears for ten-fifteen minutes, which is fine with me. Meanwhile, I have had to flag someone to get a wine list. Now we are ready to order, but have not decided on the wine.

By now our waiter is getting annoyed, because he will not be able to turn our table one more time. If it's a large wine list, it will take time to make a decision. The waiter is surprised, because my wife makes the wine decision. Now he is taking our orders, and he starts with my wife. Good start. She orders and immediately he says, "Good choice." I order veal chop. "Good choice." My wife orders a cabernet. "Good choice." I am glad he agrees with our choices. He places our orders, comes back with the wine glasses and pours a little wine in my glass for tasting. Now I am really going to yank his chain. I wait and wait. He is clueless. Finally, I tell him he should have my wife taste the wine first, since she ordered it. After her approval, he is pouring the wine, filling the wine glass three quarters full. That is a no-no.

The entrees arrive. He serves me from the right with his left hand and reaches across the table to serve my wife, ending with the famous "Enjoy!" This drives me crazy. This person never has been taught how to wait on tables. He is, at best, a delivery man. At least he could serve from the right with the right hand or serve from the left with the left hand. Very simple. The waiter will expect a 20% tip. I give him 5% and explain that it is not personal, but he should learn his profession or sell pencils on the waterfront.

Some large restaurant chains have instructed their wait staff to kneel on the front of your table or to sit next to you to take your order. Management must think that standing in front of the customer is condescending. All it shows me is that management is covering up bad service with a gimmick. This is very unfortunate. For the past twenty-five years this nation has worked very hard to improve food preparation, techniques, and quality of the raw materials. There has been a revolution in what we now have available for wines, cheeses, and bread. Sadly, service has not improved with the food.

The solution? First, have all cooking schools – and there are many more today – offer a two-year degree program in table service and oenology. And second, American customers need to learn to tip appropriately.

Christine Baird's Apple Hash

Serves 4 - 6

Prep time: 10 minutes

Cooking time: 50 – 55 minutes

The Story

Christine was a pastry chef at the New England Culinary Institute, while I was the chef at Tubb's and the bakeshop was down below. I was always calling Christine to test the special of the day, and one day she rewarded me by bringing this delicious and simple pie.

The Recipe

2 whole eggs
½ C granulated sugar
Zest of one orange
Juice of one orange
Pinch of kosher salt
4 C unpeeled shredded Granny Smith apples (about 3)
1 9-inch pie crust

Preheat the oven to 400°.

In a stainless steel bowl shred the apple, add eggs, sugar, zest, orange juice, and salt. Mix well. Pour into the pie crust. Place into the preheated oven, bake for 50 – 55 minutes.

Note: I always have a couple of commercial pie crusts in my freezer, it is very convenient and you can make a quiche or a pie when some unannounced guest arrives.

Cooking with Chef Michel

Oh no ... another cookbook! !

Cookbooks are a dime a dozen. You don't need another recipe for beef bourguignon. If you do, you can choose from dozens on the Internet.

My goal is to provide information to make you a better cook, no matter what recipe you are following.

Why do we cook food?

Cooking transforms food from its raw state, in the process changing its outward appearance, its color, its texture, its flavor, while creating aromas that stimulate the appetite. Think of your mom's apple pie or the smell of garlic walking by a restaurant. Cooking food makes it more digestible, and more palatable.

Cooking is very simple. It is what happens when you apply heat to food. You must control the heat regardless if the source is a BBQ grille, an electric stove, or a gas burner. Heat is not simply on or off. This is why we have those little things on the front called knobs. You control the heat by turning them to the right or to the left. It may seem like I am trying to be funny, but this is very basic, and too often overlooked.

You must learn how to cook food perfectly, not overcooking like my grandmother used to do, not undercooking like those al dente green beans. They might look good, but won't taste good until they reach the magic point of cooking perfection. And they will not need toasted almonds! A little butter will do nicely.

The Food:

Buy absolutely the very best food available; you don't leave it in the trunk of your car regardless of where you live. Wash what needs to be washed, such as most vegetables, and store them carefully.

Chef Alain Ducasse sells macaroni and cheese for $15 as a small dish in his take-out store in Paris. (He also sells Ben and Jerry's Chunky Monkey ice cream, proof that good food made in America can sell well in France.) Today you can buy veal glace or lamb glace in a specialty store. You can also buy chicken base and lobster base. The products are good, but you must use them properly. A vegetable reduction is thickened with a puree of vegetables – it may seem easy to thicken a sauce, but if you have not learned how to cook the carrots perfectly, you will fail. *Eh oui*. Simple as that. It is all about doing it properly.

The Knives:

Good knives are expensive but will last a lifetime. You do not need many knives, but they must be good ones. Do not let anybody use your knives; store them properly with a guard. Learn to work a 10-inch knife effortlessly. You need a paring knife, about 3½ inches, a vegetable peeler and a maybe a boning knife if you are planning to do meat. Buy knives that feel good in your hand.

Pots and Pans:

Again, quality is more important than quantity. Avoid aluminum pans. Thick copper pots are good, but I find that people hang them on the wall, rather than using them, because it makes them look like serious cooks. I prefer cast iron. They cook evenly and retain the heat. If you cook for two to six people you need:

- one omelet pan, 9"
- one sauce pot, 2 ¾ qt.
- one pot, heavy-gauge, 6 qt.
- one pot, enamel cast iron, 8 ½ qt.
- one large sauté pan 5, qt.

The Pantry:

Oh what a nightmare! First, discard all powdered spices which have been in the pantry for more than six months. They are bitter. Avoid flavored salt (such as garlic or onion), buy as many whole spices as you can (whole black pepper, cumin seed). A must is Kosher Salt and Fleur de sel de Guerande (Brittany Natural sea Salt). Buy your spices on line at terraspice.com.

You should have on hand:
- Rice
- Couscous
- Arborio rice
- Pasta
- Whole peeled tomatoes
- Clam juice
- Cannellini beans
- Tomato sauce
- Flour
- Sugar
- Vanilla bean
- Spice grinder

Freezer:
- A bottle of vodka
- 1 pint mango sorbet
- 1 pint raspberry sorbet (not sherbert)
- Shrimp 16/20
- Cod loin
- Chicken stock

Now let's start cooking, or better yet, read this, then start cooking. First, pour yourself a glass of wine. Taste and start reading.

There are two main cooking principles. The first is cooking by "sealing" with browning. This method retains all the juices and nutritive elements of foods by caramelizing their exterior surfaces over heat with or without addition of fat, as when broiling, roasting, and sautéing. The same result is achieved without browning by cooking the food in boiling liquid as when poaching eggs, fish, meat, poultry, pasta, and vegetables.

The second is cooking by "interchange" with browning. This method is used for pot roasting or braising meat, poultry, game, and a variety of meats such as lamb shank and ossobucco. The food is browned quickly in hot fat, a small amount of liquid is added, and the food is then simmered slowly on top of the stove, or covered in the oven (my preference). The slow cooking tenderizes the meat; the juices within the food are gradually released and mixed with the cooking liquid.

To roast is to cook food by exposure to direct heat. Preheat oven from 475° to 500° F to brown the surface of the roast and seal the juice inside the roast. Do not put on salt. As soon as the roast has browned completely, lower the oven temperature and baste often. Now you can add salt to the meat. When desired doneness is reached, remove from oven and let meat rest covered with aluminum foil.

Exterior heat will no longer exert pressure toward the center of the roast, and by reverse process the blood will now flow toward the outer layers of the meat, giving them an even color. At the same time, the muscle fibers, that have contracted because of the heat, expand and relax, producing a tender roast. (This material is taken from Michel Guerand's cuisine, *Gourmande*).

Salt. The Big One:

Salt is the most fundamental aspect of seasoning, because it enhances flavor. You may use salt before cooking or salted water like the ocean for green vegetables. During cooking, you can add a little sel de Guérande.

Salt and Pepper:

I would like to meet the &%#*! person who first put salt and pepper shakers on each table. Why pepper? Why not curry? Because it is not in the western culinary tradition? And how do you know how long the pepper has been in the shaker? If you want more salt on your food, add sea salt. If you'd like more pepper, use the pepper mill.

Flavor:

Flavor is the combination of three senses – taste, smell, and touch. The absence of any one of these components can make it difficult to identify food while eating it.

Taste consists of sweet, sour, salty, bitter, and, according to the Chinese, pungent.

Aroma can be floral, fruity, earthy, woody.

Texture is crisp, soft, light, or rich.

Sweet is recognized as sugar.

Sour is recognized as vinegar or lemon juice.

Bitter is found in burnt food, caffeine, chocolate, greens.

Savory is a meaty, broth-like taste.

The Mediator:

Salt will make taste balance in either direction. Various combinations of these five tastes will produce different results. In situations where two similar tastes are combined on a plate, most of the time there will be an increase in that taste. For example, adding honey to a sweet dessert will make it sweeter. Eating lemon (sour) with salt decreases the sour (such as in a margarita).

Cooking Tips

When shopping, do not let the bagger bruise your vegetables and fruits; food must be handled like a baby

Do not store onions next to potatoes; they will cause the potatoes to decay.

How can you recognize a cooked egg from a raw egg? You can make the cooked egg spin.

How to store lettuce, parsley, cilantro, etc. Fill a sink with lukewarm water, immerse the greens in the water, letting the sand fall to the bottom of the sink; remove the greens. Drain and clean the sink and fill it with ice water. Plunge the greens into the ice water for 3 to 5 minutes. Remove and drain. Then dry in a spinner. Store in a zip-lock bag. It will be good for 7 to 10 days.

Always smell fish before buying it; it should be odorless or smell like fresh cucumber.

If you do not like the smell of garlic on your finger, just rub a stainless steel spoon on your finger; rinse with cold water.

When cooking cauliflower in water; add milk and a piece of sourdough bread to avoid a bad smell.

Always cook green vegetables uncovered in a lot of salted water; the water should taste like the ocean.

Root vegetables (carrots, turnips, etc.) should be cooked slowly, covered in a small amount of water with salt and sugar.

To reheat green beans, put water, salt, and butter into a frying pan, make an emulsion and add the beans at once. Toss.

To sauté, first heat the pan. When the pan is hot, add the oil, then the meat or fish.

Steaks, chops, etc., should be brought to room temperature for a few minutes before grilling or boiling. Season at that time. Let the meat rest for several minutes before cutting. Fifteen to twenty minutes for a leg of lamb.

Store avocados in a brown bag with an apple and/or a banana.

Always store eggs with chanterelles or truffles in an air tight container; the eggs will absorb the flavor of the mushrooms and your scrambled eggs will be incredible.

If you are burned, quickly put your hand into ice water.

For small cuts, wash the cut and then elevate the limb above your heart.

Always rotate food in your refrigerator; first in, first out.

Always place a wet towel under your cutting board; wash your food before cutting it; use a very sharp knife to work effortlessly. If you are right-handed, place the food on your left side, and vice versa.

To keep milk from boiling over, put a small bread and butter plate upside down in the bottom of the pot.

Forget purchasing a pastry bag to pipe your chocolate mousse? Don't worry; take a zip-lock plastic bag, cut one corner into a "V" shape, *et voilà!*

Eggs

Eggs are the unsung heroes of cookery. As a chief ingredient or essential accessory, the egg has many characteristics.

Egg cooking is probably one of the most difficult kinds of cookery.

It takes repetition. This is probably the most bastardized cookery and the most simple. I am sure when you were in college you had your share of green, rubbery scrambled eggs. When I was touring the kitchens of Yale before I was hired, I saw a fried egg nailed to the bulletin board, and I knew immediately I could improve egg cookery. Remember the green hard-cooked eggs in the salad – yummy – and how about the omelet of your favorite dinner – cooked on the grill, flipped with a spatula. I think we can improve on that.

Fried Eggs

I found out there are mistakes made sometimes in translation. If you are in France a fried egg American style is *oeuf sur le plat* and not *frit*, because in France *frit* means deep fried; I have not seen any lately, but just in case you encounter this on a menu, ask a question, you never know.

Again, fried eggs are not made on a grill, but in a small frying pan. Melt butter and crack two eggs, cook very slowly; the white should remain white – no color on the edge. Some people choose to finish in a 250° oven, which is fine if you can't flip them over lightly, or whichever way you like them.

My favorite egg recipe uses vinegar. In France, we call it *assassin*, for good reason. After you have transferred the fried egg to a hot plate, pour 3 Tbsp of very good vinegar into the frying pan, reduce to half and pour over your eggs; the vinegar cuts the fat feeling of the eggs, a great contrast. You should try it instead of bacon, fat on fat!

Poached Eggs

Contrary to popular opinion, a brown egg is neither better nor more "natural" than a white egg; it is, in fact, usually smaller and well-filled. A fresh egg is heavy and should feel well-filled. An egg loses a tiny fraction of its weight every day by evaporation of water through the porous shell. It is easy to test the freshness of an egg by plunging it into salted water. An egg up to three days old will fall at once to the bottom, an egg three to six days old will float halfway up the water. If the egg is bad its floats horizontally on top of the water. This is why many restaurants will serve you an egg that looks more like a golf ball. Unless you can get real fresh eggs from a friend's coop you will have problems poaching eggs.

The following will help you.

Remove eggs from the refrigerator one hour before poaching them. Place them horizontally on a towel, this should allow the yolk to come to the center. Bring 3 quarts of water to simmer and add 1 Tbsp of cream of tartar, or ¼ C white vinegar. Crack the eggs into a monkey dish and slide into the water. Do not cook more than 4 eggs at a time. Cook for 2½ minutes, transfer to iced water. You should have a nice poached egg. When it is time to serve, just reheat in simmering water for 30 seconds.

The most popular poached egg dishes are:

- Benedictine
- Florentine - this is over creamed spinach, sprinkled with parmesan
- Over half a tomato cooked in oil coated with béarnaise sauce
- You can also poach the eggs in red wine and coat with red wine sauce

Hard Boiled Eggs

You would be amazed how many restaurants serve green hard boiled eggs on a chef salad. Again it is very simple to cook hard boiled eggs but you must pay attention to the timing:

Place eggs in cold water, bring to a boil and simmer exactly 8 minutes. Remove from the fire, drain the water and place in iced water. You will have the perfect hard boiled egg. Try combining sliced tomatoes and slices of hard boiled egg, coat with vinaigrette and chives. Another popular way to serve is to cut in halves lengthwise; crush the yolks and mix with diced salmon and then stuff the whites with the mixture. You can also serve it on top of stir-fried spinach, split the eggs lengthwise and coat with a good tomato sauce, sprinkle with parmesan cheese.

Scrambled Eggs

I am sure this is going to be an eye opener for you. It is not the French way; it is not my way (although it is); it is the *only* way scrambled eggs should be made. While working at the Lucas Carton in Paris the chef made us store eggs and truffles together in an air tight container. The eggs absorb the truffle flavors; you can do the same at home with chanterelles.

Whisk the eggs in a stainless steel bowl, and then place the bowl on the top of a pot filled with boiling water, making a double boiler. Start stirring and scraping the eggs with a wooden spoon or a rubber spatula until you reach the consistency of your liking, at which point you may add salt and pepper. It is very important that you add the salt *only* at that point; otherwise, it makes the eggs rubbery. Add a little heavy cream if you like your eggs smooth, and then add your favorite garnish. My favorite: chopped truffles.

Other toppings:
- Cheese – cheddar and parmesan
- Mushrooms – chanterelle
- Smoked salmon
- Artichoke
- Shrimp

For an elegant brunch with a mixed green salad, eggs are served in a hot pastry shell, fast and easy, not too messy to serve. The garnishes are endless.

But my favorite one is:

Piperade Basquaise
Serves 4
Prep time: 15 minutes
Cooking time: 40 minutes

1/3 C olive oil
1 large onion, sliced
1 can (28 oz) whole peeled tomatoes
4 whole green peppers, washed, sliced
Salt, pepper
8 eggs, beaten
8 slices Bayonne ham, aberico ham, or prosciutto

In a large frying pan heat olive oil, add sliced onion and sliced green pepper. Season. Cook until tender, add whole peeled tomatoes, crushed, and cook an additional ten minutes. In a bowl beat and season eggs, pour over tomato mixture, cook slowly while stirring constantly. Cook to the desired doneness, serve with ham on top.

Omelet

Omelet making is at once very simple and very difficult, for tastes differ regarding their preparation. Some like them well done, some just done, and others prefer almost liquid.

The eggs are beaten, seasoned, and poured into an omelet pan containing very hot butter, or vegetable oil. Stir the eggs briskly with a fork while shaking the pan back and forth in order to heat the whole omelet evenly. If the omelet is to be garnished, it should be done prior to rolling it up.

The whole process should be done speedily and it requires much practice to attain perfection. A perfect omelet should be oblong, no color, and no wrinkles. Three eggs per person is the right proportion. If the omelet is to be garnished, it should be a hot garnish i.e. onions, potatoes, or bacon. Stay away from salsa. If you are using chives or parsley, put in a lot and chop it just before making the omelet. It is delicious cold.

Grilled Sausage Rappini and Beans
Serves 4

Prep time: 10 minutes

Cooking time: 15 minutes

The Story

I do not eat potato chips or Doritos (well, *sometimes*) for snack, but sometimes at 3 o'clock in the afternoon you feel you need to eat something that will hold you until dinner, but it should not take all day to prepare. So I opened the refrigerator, looked in the pantry, and this is what I created.

The Recipe

1 chorizo sausage link

1 Tbsp olive oil

4 garlic cloves, chopped

1 bunch rappini

1 15 oz cannellini beans

Salt

Pepper

Place chorizo into a pot, cover with cold water and cook for 10 minutes. Remove then finish on the grill for 5 minutes. In a large pot put the olive oil and garlic, when you smell the garlic add the rappini which has been washed and stems cut off. Stir. Season. Cover and cook for 3 minutes. Reheat the beans.

Taste. Season. Taste.

Quick and healthy and tasty.

Cream of Mushroom Soup
Serves 4

Prep time: 15 minutes

Cooking time: 15 minutes

The Story

While teaching returning second year at Tubbs, I was always asking what they have learned on internship, because most of them had interned with very good chefs. Since I was basically writing the menu every day, it was a good exercise to learn what was available. One morning a student showed me the inventory sheet and pointed out that we had a basket of mushrooms which had passed their prime, he also told me that he learned how to make an excellent mushroom soup with the mushrooms which have reached that stage, while it was against my principles, let's try it and we will see what happens. It turned out to be an excellent cream of mushroom. One NECI employee always wanted the recipe, so here it is, Amy H.

The Recipe

2 Tbsp butter

2 onions, sliced thin

1 lb domestic mushrooms, should not be white, but
lightly sticky

Salt

1 qt water

½ C heavy cream

In a medium size pot melt the butter, add sliced onions, cook slowly until golden brown. Add the mushrooms and salt, stir and cook until the mushrooms give water. Add cold water and simmer for 10 – 15 minutes. Blend while adding the heavy cream.

Taste. Season. Taste.

Serve in hot bowls with croutons.

Cider Onion Soup Lyonnaise Style
Serves 4

Prep time: 15 minutes

Cooking time: 45 minutes

The Story

I think I have had more bad onion soup than any other kind of soup. I am always suspicious when the menu reads French Onion Soup. What makes it French? Beats me. Onion soup should not be made with chicken stock, like too many people do because they think it will taste better if it tastes like chicken. It is not to my liking! What I like about this recipe is that it is served family style and certainly fills you up. When I was on the tugboat in the Navy, you have no idea how many times officers or crew would wake me up at 2 o'clock in the morning to make that soup. Some of them had been on duty all night. Some just had a hangover. It is good for both.

The Recipe

4 oz butter

2 Spanish onions, sliced thin

2 red onions, sliced thin

1 Tbsp sea salt   Freshly ground pepper

1 quart cold water   1 bottle of hard cider

½ C heavy cream

½ baguette, sliced think and dried in the oven

½ lb Swiss cheese, shredded

In a heavy-gauge pot melt the butter, add onions and salt. Cook slowly, stirring occasionally to prevent scorching. This is what will give a nice color and lightly caramelized onion should be fully cooked before adding water and cider. Bring to a simmer and cook for 15 minutes. Taste. Season. Taste. Blend adding the heavy cream.

In an ovenproof bowl make several layers of sliced bread and cheese, then pour the onion soup over it. Bake in a 350° oven for 30-40 minutes. To serve: Place bowl in the middle of the table. Each guest should ladle his or her own soup. It can be messy to serve, but it will stay hot!

Saffron Mussel Soup

Serves 4

Prep time: 20 minutes

Cooking time: 20 minutes

The Story

In France the national dish once was "steak frites." In Belgium it is "mussel frites" with beer. Now it is so popular, they have opened restaurants only serving mussels, it is like fast food... only much better. The best time to eat mussels is between May and October. In France the most popular is "mussel mariniere". My version has saffron.

The Recipe

2 Tbsp butter
1 medium onion, diced to ¼"
4 garlic cloves, chopped fine
4 shallots, chopped fine
2 twigs of thyme   1 bay leaf
Salt, pepper
1 pinch saffron, steeped in ½ C water at 200°
½ bottle dry white wine (Muscadet)
4 lbs mussels, washed and debearded
1 C heavy cream (optional)

Clean the mussels and remove the dead or broken ones. In a large pot, melt the butter, add the onions, garlic, shallots, thyme, bay leaf. Cook slowly until translucent. Add the wine and cook for 10 minutes, add the saffron and water. Add the mussels, and cover. Shake or toss occasionally until the mussels are open. Strain the stock and reduce for 5 minutes, add the heavy cream. Taste. Season. Taste. Pick the mussels, place in a hot soup bowl. Pour the stock over.

Note: this can be served cold.

Seche Verte Soup
Serves 4
Prep time: 30 minutes
Cooking time: 15 minutes

The Story

My father-in-law René Le Goff was a great gardener, and every summer when we went to visit, he took me every day in the garden to show me his labor of love, and since I hated gardening, I really appreciated what he was doing. He even had a tool shed near a little brook so we would spend hours admiring the garden. He would tell me what he was going to grow next year on such and such a spot. He never used fertilizer, but made his own compost. I do not think he ever bought a vegetable except from February until the garden started to produce his supply again! So one day he harvested what was to be our dinner and dropped everything on the table. *Hey, Chef, see what you can do!* I love to braise cabbage, but is was summer and dinner was to be served at 7:00. I had to come up with something quick like a stir fry. I was allowed to add leftovers, and cooked navy beans. No water needed.

The Recipe

¼ C olive oil   6 garlic gloves, finely chopped

1 lb haricot vert or 1 lb French green beans

1 head savoy cabbage, outer leaves removed and sliced
    thin

1 lb fresh spinach, stemmed, washed and drained

1 bunch watercress, stemmed, washed and drained

Sea salt   Freshly ground black pepper

4 Tbsp fresh chives, chopped

In a large, heavy-gauge pot, pour oil, salt and garlic. Slowly cook the garlic. (The garlic may cook very fast. Do not brown.) Add the beans, followed by the cabbage, cook covered to lightly steam the cabbage and beans, and then add the spinach and watercress. Stir frequently. The greens should release water. Taste. Season. Taste.

To serve, present in a shallow warm soup bowl. Sprinkle with chives.

Vermont Cheddar Ale Soup

Serves 4

Prep time: 30 minutes

Cooking time: 30 minutes

The Story

You really need to make this soup on a cold Vermont day. Since we always have Vermont ale and sharp cheddar in our refrigerator, what better way to rotate the stock? Invite a couple of friends and tell them to bring some sourdough bread.

The Recipe

1 Tbsp butter
4 bacon slices, diced ¼"
1 large Spanish onion, diced ¼"
2 carrots, peeled, diced ¼"
2 Tbsp all purpose flour
1 qt chicken stock
1 bottle Vermont Ale, flat
½ C heavy cream
8 oz sharp cheddar, grated
Salt, black pepper

Melt butter, then add bacon, cook until crispy. Add onions and carrots, cook until tender. Sprinkle flour and stir well, add chicken stock and beer. Bring to a simmer and cook for 15 minutes. Add heavy cream and grated cheddar stirring constantly. Serve with sourdough bread.

Vietnamese Sour Soup
Serves 4
Prep time: 20 minutes
Cooking time: 10 minutes

The Story
My friend Jean Louis Armiand and his wife came to visit us the summer after we had met in Bolivia and I was eager to learn more from him; nothing better than a spicy bowl of soup on a hot summer day.

The Recipe
1 lb fresh ripe tomatoes, peeled and seeded (or canned)
1 lb fresh pineapple   1½ qt chicken stock
12 dry shrimp (Vietnamese style)
¼ C granulated sugar   ¼ C Nuoc nam
1 Thai chili
1 stick lemon grass, sliced thin
Salt to taste
1 bunch scallion, sliced thin
4 oz bean sprouts
Garnish – mint, cilantro, basil

Dice the tomatoes and pineapple to ¼" and place into a 3 qt sauce pan. Heat, then add chicken stock, simmer for 5 minutes. Then add all the remaining ingredients except the garnishes. Bring to a rapid boil. Serve immediately, sprinkle the garnishes on top.

Riesling Chicken Fricassee
with Cucumber and Tomato

Serves 4

Prep time: 20 minutes

Cooking time: 40 minutes

The Story

This dish was served as a weekly special at Chez Jenny" an Alsatian Brasserie in Paris where I worked after my apprenticeship. We used to make 50-60 orders served over fresh pasta. Often people ask me if you can replace the heavy cream with chicken stock. My answer is yes, but it is not going to taste as good. Also remember you do not have to have a big serving.

The Recipe

1 Tbsp oil   3 Tbsp butter

1 2½ - 3 lb broiler, cut in 8 pieces

8 shallots, peeled and quartered

1 C Riesling   1½ C heavy cream

Salt and pepper

2 tomatoes, peeled, seeded and diced

2 cucumbers, peeled, seeded and cut in 1" slices

1 lb mushrooms, quartered

In a large sauce pot, heat the oil and butter and slowly and lightly brown the chicken pieces. Discard some of the fat, add shallots and sweat them until translucent. Add the Riesling and heavy cream; return the chicken to the fire. Season and simmer until the chicken is tender. Remove the chicken and reduce the sauce to desired consistency. Sauté the quartered mushrooms and add to the sauce with the cucumbers and diced tomatoes. Reheat the sauce, Taste. Season. Taste. Add the chicken and serve on a hot plate.

Note – this can be served over linguine or rice pilaf.

Lamb Curry

Serves 4

Prep time: 25 minutes

Cooking Time: 45 minutes

The Story

Lamb and curry are two kinds of food that people either love or hate. It must be like calf liver overcooked by your mother or your grandmother. This recipe will convert you to curry at least.

The Recipe

2 lb lamb, back or shoulder, cubed 1 inch

¼ C oil

2 medium Spanish onion, diced ¼"

2 celery stalks, peeled and diced ¼"

4 Tbsp hot curry powder

1 Tbsp ground cumin	1 Tbsp coriander
1Tbsp garlic, chopped	Salt
3 C chicken broth	1 banana, diced
¼ C coconut, grated	¼ C coconut milk

1 apple, peeled and diced ¼"

Garnishes served in a bowl; chutney, yogurt, raisins, peanuts.

Do not buy already cut up lamb, because the pieces are not uniform or cut too small.

In a heavy-gauge sauce pot heat the oil and a small amount of lamb, so it browns, not boils. Remove and set aside. Discard most of the fat; add the onions and celery and cook slowly until golden brown. Add the curry, cumin, coriander, and cooked meat and cook for 3 to 4 minutes.

Add garlic and chicken broth. Season, cover and cook very slowly for 45 minutes, check doneness, then add the remaining ingredients. Cook an additional 5 minutes.

Serve over basmati rice. Serve the accompaniments in small bowls; this will help the guests adjust their curry as they like.

Osso Bianco
Serves 4
Prep time: 30 minutes – Cooking time: 90 minutes

The Story

Several years ago when braising was rediscovered every-body had *osso bucco* on the menu, not just the Italians. Some were good, some mediocre, some just had the name. It is a great dish but you must respect every step. I found this recipe in *Les petites Plats des Trois Gros* by Pierre and Michel Trois Gros, two French chefs I really admire for their perfection in simplicity. If you are tired of eating rubbery osso bucco then try this recipe.

The Recipe

4 slices of 1½" veal shank (osso bucco)
1 C dry white wine, Chablis
1 lb small carrots, peeled and cut 2" long
2 Spanish onions, sliced thick
1 bouquet garni – Leek, celery, thyme, bay leaf
1 lb potatoes cut ½" cube
Salt   6 oz sweet green peas (frozen)
8 *cornichon* (French gherkins) sliced thin
1 egg yolk   1 C heavy cream
Lemon juice   White pepper

In a heavy-gauge pot place side by side the four veal shanks, pour 1 C of Chablis and cold water, ½" above the meat. Bring to a simmer, add salt. After 40 minutes add carrots, onions and bouquet garni, then 20 minutes later add potato cubes. Cook until the meat is tender. Cook green peas in boiling salted water, drain, reserve. Remove the meat and keep warm. Remove and discard the bouquet garni. Reduce vegetable stock, then mash with a fork. Add the peas and cornichons. Remove from the fire, combine egg yolks and cream, and slowly add to the sauce, stirring constantly. Adjust the seasoning with lemon juice, salt, white pepper.

Place the shank in a soup bowl, pour the sauce over it.

Pork Butt Braised in Milk
Serves 4

Prep time: 25 minutes

Cooking time: 90 minutes

The Story

At home during the war we ate lots of potatoes. Boiled with buttermilk in winter we added broiled chestnuts, you didn't go to bed hungry. On Sunday my mother would have roast with lots of onions and potatoes and one day she added milk because she was afraid the milk would go sour. We did not have a refrigerator nor was the milk pasteurized; the result superb.

The Recipe

2 lb pork butt

2 lb Spanish onions, sliced very thin

3 cloves garlic, cut lengthwise

1 potato, peeled and sliced thin

2 oz. butter

1 C milk

Bouquet garni

Salt and pepper

Make six incisions into the pork butt and fill with garlic. Season the pork. In an ovenproof pot melt half of the butter and brown the butt on both sides. Meanwhile in a frying pan melt the remaining butter, add onions and cook until golden, add to the meat with the potato, boiling milk and bouquet garni. Cover and bake for 90 minutes, turning the meat occasionally. Remove the meat and bouquet garni. Put the onion and potato through a food mill or food processor to obtain a great sauce. Slice the pork butt pour the sauce over it.

Poached Chicken Legs in their Broth
Serves 4

Prep time: 20 minutes

Cooking Time: 20 minutes

The Story

This soup is very popular in Vietnam; the broth is delicious because it is made with a tough bird that almost looks like the road runner. You may find one in an Asian grocery store, but a free range chicken will do and is easier for western tastes. Don't be afraid by the number of ingredients.

The Recipe

1 chicken legs, split

1 leek, cleaned and sliced thin

1 carrot peeled and sliced thin

1 onion peeled and sliced thin

2 stalks lemon grass, peel back dry leaves and slice thin

3 qt. cold water or chicken stock

Salt

1 Tbsp oil

1 lb shiitake, washed and stem removed

1 zucchini, quartered lengthwise and sliced

½ lb snow peas, snapped

4 scallions, sliced   3 Tbsp garlic

3 Tbsp ginger

¼ C nuoc nam or nam pla

2 tsp chili oil

2 tsp sesame oil

½ bunch cilantro, chopped coarsely

8 mint leaves

In a large pot place chicken, leek, carrot, onion, lemon grass, salt, chicken stock or water. Bring to a simmer and cook for 45 minutes. Remove and pick chicken. Set aside.

In a medium-size pot, heat oil, add shiitake, stir, add zucchinl and snow peas, cook for 1 minute, add scallions, ginger, garlic and the strained stock. Bring to boil, add chicken, nuoc nam, chili oil, sesame oil, cilantro, mint leaves. Serve very hot.

Roasted Chicken Susan Spicer Style

Serves 4 – Prep time: 20 minutes – Cooking time: 60 minutes

The Story

Very often friends asked me what is my favorite meal. Here it is; two dozen Belon oysters with rye bread salted butter; roasted free-range chicken with new potatoes, tart tatin. The whole thing with a bottle of Pinot Noir. Most people are surprised; they expected caviar – lobster – soufflé.

I didn't think about writing a recipe until June 2008 when my friend Susan Spicer came to NECI to speak at graduation. She had a book signing; she signed one for me with a nice little note. The same night I was flipping through the book and stopped at "Roasted chicken with olives, lemon and garlic" from *Crescent City Cooking*. Unforgettable recipes from Susan Spicer's New Orleans. After reading the recipe, I knew what I would have for dinner the next day.

The Recipe

1 chicken 2½ - 3 lbs   2 lemons, quartered
12 garlic cloves, crushed and peeled
3 Tbsp olive oi   3 sprigs rosemary
Salt and pepper   3 sprigs thyme
3 medium onions, peeled and cut into 6 wedges
½ C pitted Kalamata olives

Rinse the chicken and use paper towels to pat it dry. Place half of the rosemary and half of the thyme inside the cavity, squeeze one lemon. Tie the legs together over the cavity; it will prevent the legs from over cooking. Rub the chicken with olive oil, season.

Place the chicken in a preheated roasting pan. Bake for 30 minutes. Add the onion, garlic, lemon, and sprinkle rosemary and thyme, baste the chicken. Cook another 30 minutes. Remove the chicken to rest for 10 minutes. Stir onion, lemon, and garlic, check the doneness. Onions should be lightly crisp and caramelized.

Carve the chicken, and pour the juice over the onion mixture; spoon around the chicken.

Margot Veal Blanquette

Serves 4 – Prep time: 20 minutes– Cooking time: 90 minutes

The Story

My mother's veal blanquette actually was not the classic veal blanquette that I learned in apprenticeship because she used the veal breast. She probably didn't know it was *longe de veau* and the butcher never told her. My mother's blanquette is far superior to the classic because the veal breast, with bone, is certainly much more tasty. I still remember the taste and I always try to duplicate it but have never succeeded. She probably had a milk-fed veal with no antibiotics.

The Recipe

2 oz butter	1 veal breast chop
1 onion, peeled	2 carrot, peeled
1 clove	1 bay leaf
2 twigs of thyme	2 Tbsp salt
2 oz butter	3 oz all-purpose flour
3 C reserved stock	½ C heavy cream
2 egg yolks	1 juice of a lemon
8 oz mushrooms, washed and quartered	

In a heavy-gauge pot, melt the butter and slowly light brown the veal on both sides. Drain the fat, add the onion, clove, carrot, bay leaf, thyme, salt, and then add cold water about ½" above the meat. Start to simmer very, very slowly, removing foam. Simmer 1½ hours, check doneness – the meat should fall off the bone. Remove the carrots, onions, etc. Remove the meat and keep warm.

Make the roux. In a 2-qt sauce pot, melt butter and the flour and cook slowly until it looks like wet sand, stirring frequently. Let cool, and then add reserved stock stirring with a whisk, return to the fire. Cool 10 to 15 minutes.

Taste. Season. Taste.

Combine the heavy cream and egg yolks. Add about one cup of the sauce to the heavy cream mixture, stir and add to the sauce. Do not boil; it will make the sauce curdle. Add lemon juice to your taste. Heat the oil in a frying pan, add mushrooms and cook rapidly for one minute. Add to the sauce. Pour the sauce over the meat.

Note: serve over linguine or your favorite pasta.

Shrimp in Spicy Carrot Juice with Linguine
Serves 4

Prep time : 15 minutes

Cooking Time : 20 minutes

The Story

In the mid 90s I spent a couple of weekends working with Jean Georges Vongerichten at his restaurant, "The Lafayette" in New York City. I was really interested in flavored oils he was making and the preparation of the juice sauce – it was an eye opener. Here is one of my favorites.

The Recipe

1 lb fresh linguine

2 C carrot juice

20 shrimp 16/20 peeled and deveined

1 C sweet peas, frozen

Salt

Cayenne to taste

Cinnamon to taste

Nutmeg to taste

Cook pasta in salted water to the doneness you like. Drain but do not rinse. While pasta is cooking, bring carrot juice to a simmer in a pan large enough to hold the pasta. Add cayenne, then adjust the spiciness by adding cinnamon and nutmeg. It will balance the sweetness with the spiciness. Add shrimp and cook for 2 minutes, then add the linguine and peas. Just reheat while stirring. The starch from the pasta will thicken the sauce.

Taste. Season. Taste.

Cioppino San Francisco Style

Serves 4

Prep time: 25 minutes

Cooking time: 15 minutes

The Story

Every fisherman in the world has his own fish stew and they really use the local product, the local fish, and originally they were using the fish that nobody wanted. For example in Brittany it was *cotriade*, which is conger eel, cod, mackerel, onion, potatoes, thyme. The bouillabaisse from Provence uses rockfish, crabs, fennel, onions, tomatoes, garlic, orange peel, saffron, and olive oil. This is my own version.

The Recipe

1/3 C olive oil	2 large onions, sliced
1 fennel, sliced thin	½ garlic head, chopped
Thyme	

1 24-oz can whole peeled tomatoes, crushed

1 qt. cold water	2 bottles clam juice
Pinch of saffron	Salt, pepper

12 15/20 shrimp, peeled and deveined

1 lb scallops (diver scallops)

1 lb monkfish, cut into bite-sized pieces

1 lb snapper, but into bite sizes

1 Tbsp Pernod

Steep the saffron in a cup of water which should be between 195° and 205° F; this is very important. In a pot, pour the oil and a tsp of salt. On medium heat cook the onion and fennel until translucent, then add the tomatoes, saffron, water, clam juice, garlic, thyme, salt, pepper. Simmer for 15 minutes.

Taste. Season. Taste.

Add the monkfish, snapper, scallops, and shrimps at once. Bring back to a simmer, and cook for 3 to 4 minutes. Do not overcook. Add the Pernod. Taste. Serve in soup bowls with a red pepper aioli and bruschetta.

Poached Shrimp on Potato Cake
with Green Pea Sauce
Serves 4 – Prep time: 1 hour – Cooking time: 15 minutes

The Story

Several years ago I helped Chef Frederic Morineau of the Ritz in Sarasota to do a fund raising. There were twelve Ritz chefs from all over the world. What an event. We sure didn't cut corners. This dish was originally a "Maine Lobster Tail poached in clarified butter with Potato Gnocchi, and green Pea sauce." Here is a simpler version, less time consuming. You could adapt this simple sauce to many seafood dishes.

The Recipe

2 large russet baking potatoes
2 oz butter, unsalted   2 shallots, sliced thin
1 C dry white whine (Chablis)
1½ C chicken stock or 1½ C water with 2 tsp chicken base
1½ C green peas, fresh or 1½ C frozen sweet peas
Salt   2 tsp tarragon leaves, fresh
12 16/20 shrimp, peeled and deveined

Place the potatoes in a 375° oven, bake for 50-55 minutes or until done. Meanwhile, in a small sauce pot on medium heat, melt the butter with shallots and a little salt. Cook until translucent. Add the wine and slowly reduce to half. Add the chicken stock, bring to a boil and add the green peas, cook one minute, the peas should remain green.

Pour the sauce into a blender, add butter (optional – it will make the sauce taste better), blend until smooth, reserve. Remove the pulp from the potatoes, place into a bowl and lightly mash with the back of a fork while adding small cubes of cold butter, about 1 oz or ¼ of a stick.

Divide the potatoes into 4 equal amounts and make 4 potatoes cakes using a 3½" cookie cutter or line a 3½" lid with plastic wrap, this makes it easy to unmold. Place the 4 potato cakes in a lightly oiled non sticking pan and brown on both sides. Place the shrimp in a pot of salted boiling water, cook for 2 minutes, and remove.

Serving: Place the potato cakes onto the middle of a plate, place 3 shrimp on top of each one and pour green pea sauce around, sprinkle with freshly chopped tarragon.

Sautéed Scallops with Chorizo and Chanterelles

Serves 4

Prep time: 15 minutes

Cooking time: 10 minutes

The Story

I found that seafood and sausage are a pretty good combination, like in paella: seafood, chicken. This combination with chanterelles not only looks good, but also makes your taste buds dance.

The Recipe

1 Tbsp olive oil

8 oz chorizo dry and spicy, sliced

12 diver scallops

2 lb chanterelles, brushed and dry

½ lb Italian parsley

Salt

Pepper

In a large frying pan, slowly heat the oil and chorizo slices and warm up slowly. Transfer to a hot plate, arranged around the plate in a circle. In the same fat, sauté the scallops, one minute on each side, season lightly. Place three scallops on top of the chorizo around the plate. In the same frying pan, add olive oil if necessary and sauté the chanterelle on high heat very quickly, then add the parsley. Spoon this into the center of the plate. Serve immediately.

Sautéed Scallops with Belgian Endive

Serves 4

Prep time: 10 minutes

Cooking time: 20 minutes

The Story

Fifty years ago, if someone told me to serve sautéed endive with scallops I would look at him and say, "you are crazy." Well here you have the combination of sweet, sour, and bitter.

The Recipe

2 oz butter

4 shallots, sliced thin

4 endives, sliced thin

2 Tbsp sugar

¼ C lemon juices

Salt

12 #10 diver scallops (under10 per pound)

½ bunch chives

In a large frying pan, melt the butter and bring to a light brown, add shallots and turn down the fire, cook until shallots are translucent, add the endives and sugar; cover and cook until the endives are tender. Add the lemon juice.

Taste. Season. Taste.

In a non sticking pan melt butter, place scallops in the pan, turn the heat to medium high. Cook the scallops about one minute on each side.

Season.

In four hot plates, place the endive and top with three scallops.

Sprinkle with chopped chives.

Scallops and Linguine
Serves 4

Prep time: 15 minutes

Cooking time: 10 minutes

The Story

My friend, Julie Hendrickson, invited me for dinner one night. I was sitting at the kitchen counter, sipping a single malt scotch while watching Julie cooking pasta. Suddenly she adds to the boiling pasta water the most beautiful scallops you can find. Immediately, I told her what a shame to ruin such beautiful scallops. "Relax, Chef Michel." Which I did, taking another sip of my scotch, while witnessing the amazing dish in preparation. (It is so simple to prepare and you will dazzle your friends.) But I relaxed only after I got over the process of cooking the scallops with the pasta – no doubt imbued with a certain mellowness from the scotch!

The Recipe

1 lb fresh linguine   1 Tbsp garlic, chopped

2 Tbsp ginger, grated   3 Tbsp lime juice

1 Tbsp Nuoc nam fish sauce

2 tbsp olive oil

1 C grated carrots   ½ bunch cilantro, chopped

½ bunch scallions, sliced thin

Freshly ground pepper

1 lb Diver scallops (these are the best you can buy)

In a stainless bowl, combine garlic, ginger, lime juice, fish sauce, and olive oil. Set aside. Remove the little muscle on the side of the scallops. Set aside. Bring water to a boil. Add salt (it should taste like the ocean). Cook pasta for 8 minutes, then add scallops. Cook for 2 minutes. Drain. Toss in the garlic-ginger dressing. Add grated carrots, cilantro, scallions, and black pepper. Toss. Serve at once. Or substitute shrimp for scallops and serve cold.

Sea Bass, Shiitake, Carrot, Basil
Serves 4

Prep time: 1 hour – Cooking time: 15 minutes

The Story

I made this recipe for 200 people at the Cabot House at Harvard. It takes time to do the prep but the cooking time is short. If sea bass is not available, use Chilean bass.

Sea Bass Marinade

½ C soy sauce	¼ C rice wine
¼ C sake	¼ C sugar
1 tsp garlic, grated	1 tsp ginger, grated
4 6-oz bass steaks	

Whisk all the ingredients together, cover the bass and marinate for at least 12 hours, 24 is best. Turn the fish several times so that it will marinate evenly.

The Broth

1 qt rich chicken broth	¼ C soy sauce
2 tsp ginger, minced	2 tsp garlic, minced
$^1/3$ C rice wine	$^1/3$ C rice wine vinegar
1 tsp sesame oil	

Garnish

1 C shiitake mushrooms, julienned

¼ C leeks, julienne

1 carrot, sliced very thin

1/3 C basil, julienne

The Recipe

The preparation is very time consuming but easy if you have a sharp knife and start the previous day. Make the marinade and marinate the bass. Combine the broth and garnish and simmer for 5 minutes. Remove the bass from the marinade and put under the broiler. Cook until caramelized on all sides. Pour the broth into a large soup bowl, place the caramelized bass on top.

Shrimp with Lemon Grass
Serves 4

Prep time: 20 minutes

Cooking time: 30 minutes

The Story

This dish is very light like the Vietnamese cuisine; you can serve it as soup or entrée by adding Vietnamese noodle.

The Recipe

20 shrimp 20/25 shell on

2 stalks lemon grass, chopped

8 oz baby spinach

1 carrot, peeled, sliced very thin

1 bunch pencil asparagus, cut in 1" lengths

¼ bunch cilantro   8 oz snow peas

1 small yellow squash, sliced on bias

1½ quart cold water   Salt and pepper

3+ Tbs peanut oil   Sesame oil to taste

4 oz ginger root, peeled, split lengthwise & chopped

6 oz white domestic mushrooms, washed, sliced

Peel shrimp. Save shells for next step.

In a heavy-gauge sauce pan, heat 1 Tbsp oil and shrimp shell stirring frequently until shells turn red. Add cold water and salt, simmer for 10 minutes. Add lemon grass and ginger. Turn off heat, let infuse for 10 minutes, strain, and reserve.

Clean and cut all vegetables.

Bring shrimp stock to boil, add carrot, cook 5 minutes, and then add asparagus, mushrooms, snow peas, squash, bring to a simmer. Then add all shrimp, bring back to simmer. Remove from heat.

Taste. Season. Taste.

To serve: In a large pasta bowl place raw spinach and ¼ tsp sesame oil, ladle shrimp and vegetables into bowl and serve.

Gâteau Breton

Serves 6-8

Prep time: 15 minutes

Cooking time: 45 minutes

The Story

Gâteau Breton is to Brittany what apple pie is the U.S. My father-in-law was a baker and this was one of his most popular cakes; it is always served at four o'clock with a bowl of coffee, but I prefer it for breakfast. My mother-in-law always had one on the kitchen table covered with a napkin, every time I was passing by I would cut a very small piece which at the end of the day became a big piece, but it is so good, you can't resist. Here is his recipe.

The Recipe

11 oz granulated sugar

6 egg yolks

14 oz salted butter, at room temperature

12 oz King Arthur unbleached all-purpose flour

1 tsp vanilla

1 tsp salt

1 tsp baking powder

3 Tbsp rum or cognac

1 whole egg, beaten

1 9-10" cake mold

In a stainless steel bowl mix the sugar and egg yolks until smooth, then add the butter and mix with a wooden spoon or by hand, when well mixed add the remaining ingredients except the whole egg. Place the dough into a greased mold or tin and smooth the top with a floured hand. Brush the gâteau with the beaten egg, and with the back of the fork make a lattice on top. Place into the preheated oven at 375° for 15 minutes, then turn the heat down to 350° and bake an additional 30 minutes. Remove from the oven, let cool completely before unmolding. It tastes best at room temperature.

Crêpe Ma Pomme

Serves 4

Prep time: 30 minutes

Cooking time: 30 minutes

The Story

I do not remember when and where I found the recipe, but it is a recipe I often use in restaurants. When I was at La Rotisserie Normande, Edmond, the maître d'hotel, loved it because he could show off in front of the customers. I also serve it at home when we have company. It is easy and quick, and you can make the crêpes the previous day.

The Recipe

Batter

    1½ C flour, all purpose
    ½ tsp salt
    2 tsp sugar
    2 Tbsp melted butter
    3 large eggs
    1½ C milk

Filling

    6 Macintosh apples, peeled, cored and cut into wedges
    3 oz butter
    1 C sugar
    1 jigger Calvados or apple jack
    ½ C heavy cream

In a bowl place flour, salt, sugar, melted butter, and make a well. Then add the eggs and half of the milk, stir with a whisk, incorporating all ingredients, it will look like a paste. Keep on whisking until all the lumps are gone, and then add the remainder of the milk. Let stand one hour before starting the crêpes. It may be necessary to adjust the consistency with milk or water if it is too thick.

Using a Teflon crêpe pan 4-6″ in diameter on medium heat, pour ¼ C of the batter and tilt the pan to spread the butter evenly. Cook the crêpe until you see the edge turn brown, flip the crêpe and cook and additional 30 seconds. When cooked, flip over on a napkin or clean towel. Repeat the operation, never stack the crêpes directly on top of each other or they will stick together when are hot.

In a frying pan melt the butter, add the sugar and make a light caramel, stirring constantly. Add the apple, the caramel will solidify (don't worry it will melt). Stir constantly until the apples are cooked but not mushy.

To serve: On each plate, place a crêpe. Scoop out a fourth of the apple mixture, fold the crêpe. Add the heavy cream to the caramel, reduce to a syrupy consistency. Add Calvados.and pour over the crêpe. The apples could be cooked ahead of time and used to finish the sauce at the last minute. You may choose to whip the cream and pipe it on top of the crêpe after you have poured the sauce over the crêpe.

Goat Cheese and Apple Pie

Serves 6

Prep time: 15 minutes

Cooking time: 60 minutes

The Story

Everybody is on a diet, and I love the people who order diet soda and have cheese cake for dessert, then sweeten their coffee with saccharine. This dessert will help them keep their diet balanced.

The Recipe

16 oz fresh goat cheese

¼ C sugar

2 whole eggs, beaten

2 Tbsp lemon juice

1 Tbsp salt

1 oz butter

2 Golden Delicious apples, diced ¼"

1 9" pie crust

Preheat the oven to 350°

In a frying pan, melt the butter, add the diced apple and cook until tender, add 1 Tbsp of the lemon juice, set aside. In a food processor fitted with a plastic blade, place the goat cheese, sugar, eggs, lemon juice, and salt. Mix until the mixture is smooth. Pour half of the mixture into the pie crust; sprinkle the apple on top, then pour the remaining goat cheese mixture on top. Place in a 350° oven for 1 hour. Let cool.

Raisin Oatmeal Cookies
Serves ?
Prep time: 25 minutes
Cooking time: 10 minutes

Preheat the oven to 375°.

The Story
Imitated but never duplicated. Yes, another oatmeal cookie, who needs it? This recipe is a result of a combination of several recipes and much trial and error.

The Recipe
20 oz salted butter, at room temperature
12 oz light brown sugar
8 oz sugar
3 eggs
2 tsp vanilla
1 tsp cinnamon
16 oz all-purpose flour
2 tsp baking powder
6 C oatmeal, rolled
2 C raisins

In a stainless steel bowl mix the butter, brown sugar, and sugar. Do not overmix. Add the eggs, vanilla, cinnamon, flour, and baking powder. Then fold in the rolled oats and raisins. Scale at 3 oz with an ice cream scoop. Place on a sheet pan, not too close to each other. Flatten each one with a fork. It should look like a small hockey puck. Bake at 375° for 10-12 minutes. They should be slightly soft when you remove them from the oven. Let cool then store in an airtight container.

Strawberries Romanoff

Serves 6

Prep time: 10 minutes

The Story

During the strawberry season I always had a bowl of straw-berries Romanoff on the dessert cart, I even had wild strawber-ries from June to August and even September. The scent and the flavor of really ripe strawberries is absolutely incredible, you can use either one.

The Recipe

2 pints ripe strawberries
$1/3$ C granulated sugar
$1/3$ C Grand Marnier or Kirsch
1 C heavy cream
Zest of 1 orange (optional)

Rinse the strawberries quickly if dirty before hulling them. They should never be soaked or handled too much. Cut the strawberries in ½, place in a bowl and add the sugar, Grand Marnier, and orange zest. Refrigerate for one hour maximum. In a cold bowl, whip the heavy cream to a peak, then fold in the strawberries. Serve in a chilled bowl. You can keep some of the whipped cream for piping on top of the strawberries.

Warm Chocolate Bombe

Serves 6

Prep time: 15 minutes

Cooking time: 20 minutes

Preheat the oven to 325°.

The Story

Everybody loves chocolate dessert; everything is chocolate from the ice cream to sorbet to mousse, compared to Europe where you can have as many coffee flavored desserts. A good chocolate is shiny brown. It melts on your tongue like butter, has a true aroma of chocolate rather than of cocoa powder, and is neither greasy nor sticky. The more cocoa butter it contains, the softer it is and the creamier is the chocolate. The less it contains the harder and more brittle it is. The more bitter, the more flavor it has. Unsweetened chocolate is 100% cacao, semi-sweet is 54% cacao.

The Recipe

½ lb semi-sweet chocolate

½ lb butter ½ tsp salt

3 eggs, beaten 6 oz light brown sugar

1 oz all purpose flour 2 tsp vanilla extract

Cut the chocolate and butter into small pieces, place in a stainless steel bowl over a pot of boiling water. Melt stirring frequently, when melted turn off the heat. Set aside. In a bowl place the sugar, salt, flour and vanilla slowly incorporating the eggs, then add the chocolate / butter mixing slowly until the mixture is smooth. Grease 6 ramequins, or small soufflé dishes, fill about ¼" from the top. Bake in a preheated 325° oven for 18 to 20 minutes. The center should be soft and under baked.

Bombes will soufflé lightly and just begin to crack and reveal their velvety chocolatey centers. Let set for 5 minutes. Unmold by turning it upside down on a dessert plate. You can serve as is or with a cold coffee sauce.

Recipes

Eggs and Breakfasts

Snacks and Soups

Entrées

Fish

Desserts

Index

Photographs

We are The Public Press.
You are The Public Press.

Corporate media conglomerates continue to consume independents. While ownership consolidates, new book titles, specialized cable channels, and new websites proliferate. Amidst a din of commercial noise the bandwidth and coherence of available information is narrowing. Thoughtful authors find it more difficult to find publishers for sustained, original, and independent ideas at a time when technology is making it easier than ever to disseminate information.

The casualty is free speech.

The Public Press was founded in 2004 to protect freedom of speech "word-by-word." It is a grassroots organization, beholden only to its readers, its authors, and its partners.

The goals of The Public Press are printed below:

For more information, visit ThePublicPress.com.

Empower authors.

The Public Press puts the fewest possible filters or impediments between the creator and audience. The Public does not control the publishing process in the same way that a commercial publisher does. As a result there are stylistic and quality variations from title to title. The resulting books are like hearth-baked bread or handcrafted beer compared to more uniform, but less distinctive, products of commercial counterparts.

Treat authors as partners.

The Public Press is destined to become an author co-operative, where the authors are business partners with the publisher, not licensees paid a small percentage royalty on the sales of books. The Public Press offers an alternative to the traditional author/publisher model.

Leave the lightest possible footprint.

Book publishing, historically, has been a notoriously inefficient industry from the standpoint of resource consumption. A book can travel across the country only to be returned, unsold, to its original point of shipment. The Public Press strives for economies of scale-small scale. New technologies have made available writing and editing tools, print on demand options, improved communications, and new sales outlets that make it possible for publishing to be a model of resource efficiency.

ThePublicPress.com

3849675

Made in the USA